A Ragged Mountain Press
WOMAN'S GUIDE

SEA KAYAKING

SHELLEY JOHNSON

Photographs by Doug Hayward
Series Editor, Molly Mulhern Gross

Ragged Mountain Press
Camden, Maine

New York • San Francisco • Washington, D.C. • Auckland • Bogotá
Caracas • Lisbon • London • Madrid • Mexico City • Milan • Montreal
New Delhi • San Juan • Singapore • Sydney • Tokyo • Toronto

Look for these other Ragged Mountain Press Woman's Guides

Backpacking, Adrienne Hall
Snowboarding, Julia Carlson
Mountaineering, Andrea Gabbard
Fly Fishing, Dana Rikimaru

Sailing, Doris Colgate
Canoeing, Laurie Gullion
Skiing, Maggie Loring
Snow Sports, Iseult Devlin

• •

International Marine/
Ragged Mountain Press

A Division of The McGraw·Hill Companies

10 9 8 7 6 5

Copyright © 1998 by Shelley Johnson.
All rights reserved. The publisher takes no responsibility for the use
of any of the materials or methods described in this book, nor for
the products thereof. The name "Ragged Mountain Press" and the
Ragged Mountain Press logo are trademarks of The McGraw-Hill Companies.
Printed in the United States of America.

Library of Congress Cataloging-in-Publication Data
Johnson, Shelley, 1954–
      A ragged mountain press woman's guide: sea kayaking / Shelley Johnson.
         p.   cm.
      Includes index.
      ISBN 0-07-032955-9
      1. Sea kayaking. 2. Boating for women.   I. Title.
   GV788.5.J64   1998
   797.1'224—dc21   97-48613
                                                              CIP

Questions regarding the content of this book should be addressed to:
Ragged Mountain Press
P.O. Box 220, Camden, ME 04843

Questions regarding the ordering of this book should be addressed to:
The McGraw-Hill Companies
Customer Service Department
P.O. Box 547, Blacklick, OH 43004
Retail customers: 1-800-262-4729
Bookstores: 1-800-722-4726
www.raggedmountainpress.com

Printed by Quebecor Printing Company, Fairfield, PA
Edited by Cynthia Flanagan Goss; Kathryn Mallien
Design and page layout by Carol Inouye, Inkstone Communications Design
Project management by Janet Robbins
Production assistance by Mary Ann Hensel and Shannon Thomas
Photos on pages 11, 17, 27, 39, 56, 78, 109, 134, 149 and 153 by Joel Rogers
Photo on page 145 by Jamie Bloomquist/Outside Images
Illustrations by Elayne Sears

•••••••••••••••••••••••••••••••••••••

"I couldn't believe how easy it was; so much easier than I ever imagined. Just hop in and go. I know I'm only a beginner, but I paddled out of this harbor and along the shore looking at stuff in a whole new way. It was amazing. I can do this!"

—novice kayaker Sally Lermond,
after her first time in a sea kayak

•••••••••••••••••••••••••••••••••••••

Foreword

"Big sea, little boat, out to sea I go," I chanted to myself on a white-knuckle crossing of Muscle Ridge channel. Battling four-foot waves and hoping not to capsize, I gripped my paddle with all my 26-year-old nerves. My companion and I had started too late in the day, and the wind was up. As I followed my friend's yellow kayak across the broad expanse, I measured my future in paddle strokes: one more, one more, one more. I nearly kissed the sand after landing on the island beach, and even a night spent far too close to the blare of a foghorn seemed like a redemption of sorts.

My first years sea kayaking were marked by a lot of enthusiasm but little knowledge. And an excess of baggage—and I'm not talking about the kind checked curbside. For me, new physical endeavors summon a large committee of internal experts telling me all the reasons I might not be able to cross the channel . . . complete the 10-mile paddle . . . lift the kayak onto my roof rack. The loyal committee had found its way onto my sea kayak that summer afternoon and was doing its best to halt my passage midchannel. Luckily, as I've aged I've gotten to know my internal critics and have even found ways to silence them. Gaining experience and expertise is a great way to quiet that committee, and I've found that reading about a sport and women who've tried it fosters my confidence even further. *Sea Kayaking: A Woman's Guide* is the first of an exciting new line of outdoor books—The Ragged Mountain Press Woman's Guides—written to provide you with that kind of expertise.

Sea Kayaking: A Woman's Guide teaches sea kayaking the way you'd be taught in a women's clinic, and the way I wish I'd been taught. I remember vividly the fear in the pit of my stomach when instructed (by my male partner) to "just turn the kayak over and get out." Later, the bruises on my legs told of my underwater struggle to wriggle free of the small cockpit. My friend and instructor had no clue that I was scared to death of being strapped upside down, underwater, in my kayak. And I had no idea my fears were perfectly normal. I just thought I had a case of nerves. I also figured the best solution was to turn the boat over and get the hell out. Fast. Of course I was too intimidated (and stubborn, I'll admit) to ask for advice, so I learned the hard way how *not* to get out of a capsized kayak (see page 59 for the kind of advice I wish I'd had!). But that experience—and similar ones in other outdoor activities (like the first time I in-line skated without knowing how to stop)—sent me on a search for instructional books that approached learning the way I do. I wanted books that recognized my concerns and questions and showed people like me participating in the sport. But my search was futile: I found no sea kayaking books addressing fear of capsizing or being stuck upside down in the boat, nor did I find any books telling how a 5'1" person might manage to hoist a sea kayak on and off the car by herself. Confirming that necessity is the mother of invention, I set out to create a series of books designed to teach and share outdoor advice in a manner that respects how women learn and grow—and silences our internal committees of critics (or at least puts them in their place!).

What's so different about the way women learn? If you're like me you like to hear a description of a move or tactic before launching into it. I guess you could say I'm a fan of the "talk it over and think it through first" school of outdoor learning. It gives me a chance to ask questions before I'm asked to turn my boat over. I also like to hear advice from someone like me, someone I know and trust. And I like to learn in a group so I can hear other folks' questions—and know I'm not the only one wondering which end of the boat is the bow (see page 28!). We've done our best to mimic these learning conditions in The Ragged Mountain Press Woman's Guides. Here you'll find lots of woman's voices: your instructor's, of course, but also voices of women from all walks of life who love the outdoors. *Sea Kayaking: A Woman's Guide* provides solutions, advice, and stories from women who have done what you are about to do: learn to sea kayak. I hope Shelley's words and approach help get you out to explore and enjoy, by yourself or with a friend. I'll look for you out there.

When you get a break from sea kayaking, drop us a note and tell us how we're doing and how we can improve these guides to best suit you and your learning style.

MOLLY MULHERN GROSS
Series Editor, The Ragged Mountain Press Woman's Guides
Camden, Maine
April 1998

An avid outdoorswoman, Molly Mulhern Gross enjoys running, hiking, camping, sea kayaking, telemark skiing, in-line skating, and biking and has just started snowboarding. She is Director of Editing, Design, and Production at Ragged Mountain Press and International Marine.

Contents

Acknowledgments	8
Introduction	9
What defines sea kayaking?	9
About this book	10
Chapter 1: The Female Sea Kayaker	11
A good match for women	12
How and why they got started	12
Finding your own style	14
Chapter 2: Getting Started	17
Starting out right	18
Other options for getting started	21
How does it feel?	22
Common concerns	22
Chapter 3: Getting Friendly with Your Boat	27
Naming of the parts	27
Getting adjusted	29
Carrying your boat	30
Getting your boat on and off a vehicle	32
Getting in and out	35
Balance and the art of staying upright	37
Chapter 4: Paddle Strokes and Controlling Your Boat	39
Getting to know your paddle	39
Paddle strokes	41
Chapter 5: Essential Skills for Getting Away From It All	56
The wet exit	57
Gear to get you back in	59
The solo reentry	61
The assisted reentry	66
The Eskimo roll	74

CONTENTS

Chapter 6: Your Equipment   78

Kayaks   79

Paddles   90

Safety equipment and accessories   93

Clothing as safety gear   99

Care and feeding for equipment   103

Chapter 7: Putting It All Together   109

Staying on course   109

Waves   110

Wind   113

Tides and tidal currents   118

Using the land: eddies in the ocean   122

Weather   123

The surf zone   129

Rules of the road and reality   132

Chapter 8: Hit the Water Trail   134

Navigation   134

Packing your kayak   140

A word about water trails   142

A low-impact vessel   143

Chapter 9: Tips and More Tips   145

Stretches for paddlers   145

To pee or not to pee   148

Paddling while pregnant   148

Bring along the family   149

Paddling with a disability   151

Chapter 10: Resources   153

Index   159

Acknowledgments

Writing this book was not a solo project. From my first navigation lesson some twelve years ago to the finishing touches on this manuscript, I've received a wealth of support and assistance from many. Thanks to all the women paddlers who were so generous with their time, expertise, and support of this book: Joanne Turner of Southwind Kayak Center; British Canoe Union instructor Linda Legg; *Canoe & Kayak Magazine* publisher Judy Harrison; Judy Moyer of Pacific Water Sports; Tamsin Venn, publisher of *Atlantic Coastal Kayaker*; Deb Shapiro of The Kayak Centre; Pam Sweeney of Winnipesaukee Kayak Company; all the women who were willing to be interviewed and allowed me to eavesdrop on them at various paddling events; and to all my sea kayak students over the years who've taught me so much.

Special thanks to Cheryl Levin of Maine Sport Outfitters and Ann Carroll of Far Horizons for their superb modeling of skills for the book's photographs; and to Sally Perkins for her cheerful willingness to participate. To Doug Hayward and assistant Jim Dugan: It is a rare treat working with accomplished photographers who also are accomplished paddlers. Thanks also to Nick and Lisa Dyslin (and their dog Agatha) who insisted on a weekend respite and getaway at a critical point; Derek Hutchinson and Ken Fink for their thoughtful suggestions and sometimes quite humorous point–counterpoint; and Captain Jim Sharp for nurturing my fascination with the sea and teaching me what seamanship is all about.

The Ragged Mountain Press editors and designers deserve a huge thanks for all their work: Series Editor Molly Mulhern Gross for creating, developing, and pursuing the vision of these Ragged Mountain Press Woman's Guides and for having faith in my participation; Kate Mallien and Cynthia Flanagan-Goss for their thorough and excellent editing; Jeff Serena for his enthusiastic support and openness; and Janet Robbins for her helpful suggestions and professional steering of the design process.

And finally, to my husband, Vaughan Smith, whose kayaking expertise and critical eye have been invaluable to me: Thank you for never allowing me to simply write what had already been written and for all your quick responses when I peppered you with questions and then ungratefully questioned your answers.

Why write a book on sea kayaking for women? Because I wish I'd had one when I got started. Such a book would have proven useful and reassuring. Plus, it would have been just plain fun to view the sport from a woman's point of view. You see, I believe there is a difference in how women approach new information and learn new skills—and even why they approach new pursuits at all. Sea kayaking, for one, could use a new approach.

Stories of sea captains and brave explorers pervade the world of sea kayaking. In its infancy as a sport, sea kayaking was another way for the mighty to challenge the elements and explore dangerously remote regions. I listened to tales of horrible crossings and of deprivations on long expeditions for the lessons they imparted. But this chest beating did not relate to my interest in sea kayaking. I didn't come to this sport to challenge anything. I craved peace and quiet and the incredible experiences available from the cockpit of my very own boat. Yes, the sea is demanding and capable of taking the lives of the ill prepared. But it can also offer calm reassurance to those seeking quiet and depth in their lives.

When you sit in the cockpit of your boat, you are at eye level with the world around you: a curious harbor seal, a magnificent sea cliff of forbidding granite, the horizon line as the sun breaks free for the day. This vantage point is breathtaking in its intimacy. There are no motors, no railings around you. Just a thin wall of material separates your lower body from the water, and you experience the temper of the water as you paddle or sit quietly at rest.

In sea kayaking, there are no trails or tracks to follow. You decide where you want to go and how fast you want to get there. With a few inches of water to float your boat, you can be on your way. You may paddle a few minutes from shore to enjoy your morning coffee in solitude, or you may click off mile after mile to reach an island destination. You may poke around the backwaters of a salt marsh, or you may scream down the face of a wave. It's your boat and your choice. This is the sport of sea kayaking I love so dearly.

WHAT DEFINES SEA KAYAKING?

Sea kayaking was originally a mode of transportation for people and goods and a way of gathering the ocean's rich store of food that a barren land could not supply its inhabitants. Today, the only elements that define sea kayaking are the combination of paddler, paddle, and kayak and the act of exploring a waterscape that is not defined as technical whitewater. Sea kayaking does not even require the sea. Enthusiasts explore rivers, lakes, ponds, and blackwater swamps. Sea kayaking can be done alone. It can also be done by couples, families, and entire groups of paddlers setting out together for a day's excitement.

In the last decade, there has been a move to rename the sport *kayak touring*. This name doesn't suggest a need for salt water. And from a marketing standpoint, *kayak touring* does not sound like an intimidating pursuit. But the term "touring" brings to mind heavy luggage and tedious planning—not the romance of the sea. Even those paddling landlocked waterways can imagine the lure of the sea and know this environment produced the first kayak.

In this book, I will continue to use the term *sea kayaking*. But my definition is inclusive, not exclusive. There are too many places to explore to limit ourselves to the traditional sea environment. There are too many side pursuits that can be coupled with kayaking, such as surfing and scuba diving, to define ourselves as "tourers" only. This is the real challenge of sea kayaking: defining it without restricting its practice and enjoyment.

The only limits are those determined by our own skill level, knowledge of paddling conditions, possession of suitable equipment, and—of course—the willingness to accomplish what we set out to do.

ABOUT THIS BOOK

This book is for novice, intermediate, and advanced kayakers alike. No matter your level of expertise, you will find in these pages ways to strengthen your approach to sea kayaking.

I will tell you how to get started in the sport, introduce you to sea kayaking equipment and its handling, and help you develop the skills and techniques you need to head out on the water in your own boat.

Sea kayaking ". . . is not an easy sport," attests Tamsin Venn, editor and publisher of *Atlantic Coastal Kayaker*. "It requires judgment and stamina. But being way out from land in a little boat is a remarkable challenge with limitless rewards for the prepared."

This book can help you gain those limitless rewards. I will give you the tools you need to develop good judgment and a keen eye for the details that make each outing enjoyable and safe. As your skill level expands, you will feel more comfortable in a wider range of conditions. As your understanding of paddling conditions grows, you will be able to make informed decisions about where, when, and even whether to paddle. As you gather the right equipment to paddle comfortably and safely on different kinds of water, your possibilities as a sea kayaker will be even greater.

In this book you will also meet other women who have made kayaking an important part of their lives. Their voices are woven throughout the text. From novices to veteran sea kayakers, these women share their insights about this wonderful sport—a sport whose beauty and complexity continually unfold as you mature as a paddler.

Chapter 1

THE FEMALE SEA KAYAKER

My first outing in a sea kayak was memorable.

I didn't have a clue how to control the boat. I desperately pressed on rudder pedals that were jammed in a cocked position and kept me lurching off course. My death grip on my paddle was so strong my forearms began to cramp and my upper arm muscles trembled. At one point during this two-day trip, my lower lip trembled and I had to fight back tears when the rest of the group began to pull away.

And then I got angry. I wanted my first crossing to be fun. Instead, poor planning and the rush to meet a timetable were making it miserable. But I knew I could finish the crossing in spite of the wind and the seas. And I did.

Despite a rocky start, I was drawn to this sport and determined to pursue it. Controlling my own small vessel on open water and charting my own itinerary were immensely satisfying. I wanted to try everything with my kayak—from surfing to birdwatching. I was rarely disappointed with the outcome.

Within two years, sea kayaking was my livelihood. I began guiding, instructing, and organizing sea kayaking programs along the coast of Maine. Sea kayaking, combined with writing and teaching, continues to be my livelihood. It is also my means of relaxation as I explore the many waterscapes that fascinate me.

But I always remember my first outing in a sea kayak and realize that it didn't have to be that way. This book can help you avoid a rocky start.

A GOOD MATCH FOR WOMEN

> " **T**his is a sport that requires technique. Women tend to be better listeners, so they develop better technique."
>
> —Judy Harrison, paddle sports advocate and publisher of *Canoe & Kayak Magazine*

Women are well suited to sea kayaking. Your skill as a kayaker does not depend on your height, muscle mass, or upper body strength. (You might power your way through a day of paddling on brute strength alone, but you probably won't have much fun!) What you do need to be a skilled sea kayaker are an eye for detail, an aptitude for planning, the willingness to hone a particular technique, and a reasonable sense of balance. It is not surprising, then, that recent statistics reveal that close to half of the kayaking population is female.

When it comes to physical makeup, women are blessed with a lower center of gravity than most men. This is helpful for boat balance and control. Women also tend to be more flexible than men. This is useful when you are trying to keep a rocking boat centered under you and you must let your hips swing with the boat's motion. When it comes to learning proper technique, experienced paddler and paddlesports publisher Judy Harrison explains it best: "This is a sport that requires technique. Women tend to be better listeners, so they develop better technique."

HOW AND WHY THEY GOT STARTED

Certain traits common among women may make them well suited to sea kayaking. But women who are active in the sport are drawn to sea kayaking for a myriad of reasons, and the how and why of their beginnings are all different.

Sea kayaking brought some women to new parts of the world.

Joanne Turner was drawn to the idea of traveling long distances over the ocean. She started out using a touring kayak to "backpack island to island on the rocky coast of Maine," she says. "I fell in love, both with that coastline and with touring kayaks." When she went home to California, Joanne spent her first 300 miles over six months paddling alone in the calm waters of Newport Bay. Joanne remembers one afternoon, when "I decided to head out the breakwater to sea. But I found the swells of the ocean so intimidating that I literally backed up and returned to the safety of the harbor. I didn't even feel comfortable turning around for fear I would capsize. Little did I know that fourteen short months later I would be paddling solo for several weeks along the southern coast of China!" Now a veteran kayak instructor, Joanne is co-owner of Southwind Kayak Center in Irvine, California.

Judy Harrison has covered thousands of miles, from Labrador to Alaska. For her, "Sea kayaking should not be intimidating. It is simply transportation—transportation that has been

Linda Legg explains the fine points of paddling technique. (Courtesy of Linda Legg)

Joanne Turner enjoys tropical paddling off Iriomote Island, Japan. (Courtesy of Southwind Kayak Centre)

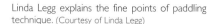

Judy Harrison explores a favorite stretch of wilderness by kayak. (Courtesy of Dave and Judy Harrison)

around for thousands of years in the harshest environment." Judy, who has canoed for over 40 years, moved to the Seattle area over 21 years ago. There, "Sea kayaks were being promoted as a means to enjoy the shoreline and to become familiar with aquatic birds and mammals," she remembers. As wilderness trippers, she and her husband Dave explored a different type of wild environment in this new type of boat.

When she saw her first sea kayak at age 36, Linda Legg—now a kayak instructor and guide—was intrigued by the adventure a touring kayak offered. She remembered her teenage days canoe camping in the Adirondacks. "I thought that I would be able to go kayak camping in a similar way and have similar good times—which turned out to be true."

" **I**'m a classic Type-A personality. I know how to spell the word relax, but it's not something I do very often. When I get in a sea kayak and leave the shore, it's one of the few times that I can really enjoy the ultimate escape—away from faxes, phones, voice mail, and time commitments."

— Deb Shapiro, co-owner of The Kayak Centre

For other women, kayaking is a way to combine different interests.

Jean Davis wanted a way to birdwatch and explore the placid waters around her waterfront home. She was taken with the ease of a small kayak. It was stable and comfortable and a relatively inexpensive way to enjoy the water.

Sailing enthusiasts and first-time kayakers Cathy Bertram and Priscilla Anson, who were looking for another way to get on the water and get some exercise, find the appeal of kayaking to be the serenity and quiet. And for Deb Shapiro, co-owner of The Kayak Centre in Wickford, Rhode Island, it is an ultimate escape. "I'm a classic Type A personality. I know how to spell the word relax, but it's not something I do very often. When I get in a sea kayak and leave the shore, it's one of the few times that I can really enjoy the ultimate escape—away from faxes, phones, voice mail, and time commitments."

FINDING YOUR OWN STYLE

As you've learned from these women, sea kayaking is flexible enough to change with each paddler's goals and moods. It is one of few sports that can accommodate so many broad interests. What mode of sea kayaking suits your style?

Have kayak, will travel

Pat is always ready for her next trip. Her gear is organized in color-coded dry bags and her well-used sea kayak lives on the roof of her car. She also owns an inflatable kayak, which stows in a backpack, that she can bring on an airplane or carry on a hike to a launch site.

Pat has explored the coast of Maine, Baja, Vancouver Island, Alaska's Prince William Sound, and her home waters of Puget Sound. She is planning a three-week expedition to New Zealand.

Pat began kayaking by tagging along with a local paddling group—aping their movements and keeping quiet for fear they'd realize how little she knew. She learned by experience and had a few close calls along the way. Pat is tough and practical. She is comfortable spending hours a day in her boat, and she doesn't think twice about dropping out for days at a time to explore unknown waters.

The naturalist

Anne owns a small kayak and roams the lakes, ponds, and bogs around her New Hampshire home. She is an avid birdwatcher. Anne chose one of the widest kayaks available and doesn't worry about its lack of speed or storage capacity. She can set up a spotting scope in her large cockpit and birdwatch from the water, which she believes is less threatening to the birds. Anne often packs a lunch and spends most of the day exploring.

For years, Anne canoed with her husband and their three children. She was always the one who wanted to sneak off and explore on her own, so she is ecstatic about having her own boat on the bank of her lakeside home. She uses her boat during the warm months only, about three days a week on average.

The tourist

Jeannie doesn't own a boat, but she plans her annual vacation around a sea kayaking adventure. She prefers to have someone else plan all the details, so she makes reservations with an outfitter each year to explore the areas that interest her.

A new kayak and some of the safety gear and accessories all kayakers should consider.

Jeannie's excursions have ranged from five days to two weeks and from Baja to Belize. She prefers some luxury, with stayovers at a bed and breakfast, but she is also comfortable camping out for several days at a time. Until last year, Jeannie had only used a double kayak on her excursions. Her next vacation will include three days of formal instruction in a single before taking off to explore.

Mom, the kayaker

Linda, a single mom, uses a sit-on-top (a kayak with no deck) double kayak for her family outings. It's cheap, fun, and sometimes the only way she finds time to get outside!

Linda yearns for her own sleek single. But she admits that, with the kids, she probably wouldn't use it much. Her four-year-old son nestles down in front of her, and her seven-year-old daughter gamely paddles from the bow position. Linda can easily reach both children at any time from her stern position, and she has no trouble controlling the boat as a solo paddler. Linda originally tried the boat when she stumbled across a free demo day at a local park, where she had taken the kids for an outing. On calm days, she throws the boat into the back of her pickup truck and heads to the protected waters of the salt marshes near her Rhode Island home.

The athlete

Donna is always doing something active. She mountain bikes, skis, runs—and she paddles. She originally got her kayak because several of her friends had them. It was great fun to plan weekend trips or just paddle after work. Now, she also uses her kayak for fitness.

Donna has a set course across the lake and back that gives her a 35-minute aerobic workout. She likes the feel of flying across the water, and she has begun to pay more attention to her paddling technique. She recently took her boat surfing and thought it was an absolute blast, even though she swam quite a few times. What she'd really like is a faster, fiberglass kayak (she now owns a plastic model) and a small sit-on-top model for surfing.

Half of a couple

Laura never really planned to become a kayaker. But her husband Mark was excited about giving it a try, so she went along. Laura and Mark took a weekend course together, and she was hooked!

Still, Laura had doubts about keeping up with Mark if she was in a single, and she didn't want to deal with his impatience if he had to keep waiting for her to catch up. So they bought a double kayak. Laura loves the feel of the double as it plows through the water. She also has this hilarious image of herself as the figurehead on the bow of some grand vessel at sea.

She and Mark are planning a week-long paddle along the coast of Maine and are considering an Everglades trip next spring.

You've heard how other women got started, and you've learned how well sea kayaking can be adapted to different circumstances and interests. Now, as veteran kayaker Judy Harrison says, "Master the basic paddling skills, use a little common sense, and go have fun!" It's your turn.

Chapter 2

GETTING STARTED

Before you jump into a sea kayak, take time to consider what you want out of the sport. Because sea kayaking is so diverse and offers so many options, you need to develop your focus first. As you gain confidence in your paddling skills and understand how much the sport can offer, your goals may shift. That's okay. Sea kayaking is a sport that will grow with you.

To begin, ask yourself the following questions.

- What do you want to be able to do immediately?

- What will you primarily use your boat for?

- Where will you do most of your paddling?

- Is there something (maybe it's just a fantasy at this point) you'd love to do once you become more skilled?

- Is there a sport or hobby (scuba diving, fly fishing, photography, etc.) you do now that you can use your kayak to enhance?

As you read through the upcoming chapters on technique and equipment, keep your answers to these questions in mind. That way, you can take each new piece of information you gain and use it to flesh out your plans and clarify your goals.

STARTING OUT RIGHT

The best way to start is to get instruction from a qualified paddling instructor. "Listening to an instructor is really the fastest and most successful way to learn," says veteran kayaker Joanne Turner. Even if you have a friend who would be willing to let you try her boat, go to a professional instructor to learn the skills.

A day of instruction will provide you with invaluable safety information and some basic paddling skills—skills you won't have to correct later on.

Novice kayaker Lynne Mahoney saw firsthand the value of getting professional instruction first. "I'm glad I signed on for a kayaking class," she says. "Some of my friends just started on their own, and they seem to struggle to keep their boats going where they want them to. I'm not very strong, but my instructor explained ways to use all of my body to control the boat."

An investment in professional instruction will also make you better informed when it comes to making equipment buying decisions. After a day of instruction, you will feel more comfortable in any boat and will understand how to compare different features and designs. A boat that felt tippy at 9:00 in the morning might feel rock-solid stable later that afternoon!

Finding a course of instruction

Check the course offerings at your local paddling shop or outfitter. Try to talk to the instructor before signing up for a class and explain what type of paddling you want to do. Keep in mind your answers to the questions at the opening of this

". . . Women come with a much more open mind to learning technique than many men do so they often learn more quickly. They are less invested in the way someone else showed them or the way they figured it out on their own. Listening to an instructor is really the fastest and most successful way to learn. Women often can do that easily!"

—veteran instructor Joanne Turner,
Southwind Kayak Center

" I'm glad I signed on for a kayaking class. Some of my friends just started on their own and seem to struggle to keep their boats going where they want them to. I'm not very strong, but my instructor explained ways to use all of my body to control the boat. I feel sure of myself in calm water and maybe a little bit of wind. Some day I might like to try some rough water."

—new kayaker Lynne Mahoney

Having an instructor demonstrate proper techniques is the best way to learn.

chapter and mention any concerns you have about accomplishing your goals. Here's a list of questions you should ask before signing up for an instructional program:

- What is the instructor-to-student ratio? Anything exceeding a 1:6 ratio is too high, limiting your access to the instructor and the amount you can learn in a day.

- Are there concerns about cold water temperatures? If so, will I be provided with a wetsuit or drysuit, or will I need to rent or provide my own?

- Will I get a chance to observe and practice ways to get back into my boat after a capsize (solo and assisted reentry techniques)? If not, when and how can I get this experience?

- What training or certifications does the instructor have? Certifications from the British Canoe Union or American Canoe Association mean the instructor has met the standards of the organization and has some instructional experience.

- Will there be different models of boats available in class to fit different-sized people?

- Do I need to bring my own lunch, snacks, or water bottle?

- Do I need to carry in my boat everything I need for the day? If so, will water-proof bags be provided?

- Where will the class be held? Will I have the chance to paddle on any open water, or will the entire class be held on a small pond or in a pool?

- Who determines a class cancellation due to bad weather? Must I reschedule, or will I receive a refund?

- After my first class, are there other courses or methods of instruction they might suggest?

- Are there any incentives with boat purchases? Often, paddlesports dealers offer some sort of instructional package for those buying a boat.

- If I have a disability, what adaptations will be made to the equipment? When will these be done?

Women's-only courses

Many women feel more comfortable in a course with other women. As a result, many shops and outfitters offer women's-only sea kayaking courses. If your local outfitter doesn't offer such a course, you always have the option of gathering your own class and buying out a particular date. British Canoe Union (BCU) instructor Linda Legg believes it's easier for women to learn kayaking in an all-women's class. "Women, in my experience, like to learn new skills in small chunks—not all at once. They prefer new skills broken up into little chunks and warming up to it rather just diving in," she says.

Linda has also observed how much talking about learning is for women a part of learning. When learning different moves, "[Women students] talk before they do it. Then they talk about it afterwards—their impression of it. Then other women will share what they experienced. It's a group thing."

In my experience, women often learn physical movements in a different fashion than men. I have observed that women request more verbal explanation and ask to see a move repeated more often than male students. Rather than trying a move unattended, women students often ask me to

All-women instructional programs are a popular choice, to get started or to brush up on skills.

lead them through a move so they can "feel" what is expected. Since women usually cannot rely on brute strength to see them through, it is imperative that they learn each movement correctly.

Even though women and men might have different learning styles, I believe women can receive excellent instruction in both mixed classes and women's-only classes. A good instructor can present information in a variety of ways to get through to every student.

What to expect on the first day of school

The best way to prepare for your first kayaking class is to relax and bring an open mind. Other students often bring their own questions and fears. You can learn a lot by simply listening and observing your fellow students and your instructor. If you wear glasses, attach a retainer strap to them. Pack a water bottle, sunscreen, and some quick snack food in waterproof packaging. And don't forget to ask lots of questions!

On the first day of instruction, you should learn how to get in and out of your boat from a variety of launch sites. You should also learn what safety gear you should have with you and how to use it. A good instructor will model, dissect, and critique every stroke she is teaching you, and she should be able to help you smooth out the rough spots in your strokes.

Plan on getting wet your first day in the boat. You should get a chance to practice several wet exits (getting out of the boat after you capsize). You should also learn how to reenter your boat from the water, both with and without the help of another kayaker.

Make sure to bring the right clothing for the class so you are comfortable in and out of the water. Except in regions with warm water temperatures (above 75°F/24°C), you will be more comfortable in a wetsuit or drysuit—especially when practicing wet exits and reentry techniques (see Chapter 6 for more on kayaking apparel). Instructors in cold water regions will require you to have proper protection from the water, and they may provide a wetsuit or drysuit as part of the class fee or have them available for rental.

A good instructor will never push you beyond your capabilities. But she may nudge you to keep you focused and keep you on a learning curve. If you are uncomfortable with a piece of equipment or with the execution of a particular movement, tell your instructor. Discomfort can often be corrected with a minor adjustment in equipment or with a different explanation.

There may be a lot of information to digest on the first day of school. You should come away from a day of instruction with a solid understanding of why the boat does what it does in certain conditions. As you spend more time on the water, you'll probably find yourself saying, "So that's what she was talking about!" Put all these pieces of information together, and go have fun. Don't hesitate to take another course.

OTHER OPTIONS FOR GETTING STARTED

Some women prefer to try kayaking by going on a guided trip. Shorter tours offer an easy sampling of sea kayaking, and they might be just the ticket if you want to give the sport a quick try.

Most outfitters welcome beginners, and they will cover basic safety information and paddling skills over the course of the tour. On such a trip, however, you will not receive the individual attention that an instructional program would provide. Guided tours focus more on the scenery along the way rather than on paddling techniques. Still, a guided tour is loads of fun, and it can give you a good feel for a particular paddling area.

You can also educate yourself by visiting paddling shops and asking questions. Don't worry: The staffs of these shops are used to it! Read paddling magazines (see the Resource section, page 153, for more on publications). Find out if there is a paddling club or informal paddling group in your area. Many clubs have boats you can try. Clubs are also a good source of information about local paddling spots and a great way to meet other paddlers of many skill levels. Ask lots of questions and keep an open mind.

HOW DOES IT FEEL?

Imagine a slow hula or a sinuous Elvis Presley the first time you sit in a kayak. Your boat will naturally wobble and move with the motion of the water. This is good—a boat that moves fluidly with the water will take care of you in a variety of conditions. You will also need fluid movements. Relax and let your hips swing with the boat's motion. If you're stiff and can't unlock your hips, you will feel less stable. Every twitch and movement of the boat will then be magnified by your upper body instead of being absorbed by your lower body.

As novice kayaker Sally Lermond found, getting in a kayak for the first time can be an exciting experience. "I couldn't believe how easy it was. . . . Just hop in and go. I know that I'm only a beginner, but I paddled out of this harbor and along the shore looking at stuff in a whole new way. It was amazing. I can do this!"

With your first paddle stroke, you too will be pleasantly surprised at how easy it is to accelerate your boat and how helpful it is to have two blades on your paddle as you alternate strokes on either side of your boat. Enjoy the sensation of being part of the water and feel the boat respond to each paddle stroke. You're on your way.

> "I couldn't believe how easy it was; so much easier than I ever imagined. Just hop in and go. I know I'm only a beginner, but I paddled out of this harbor and along the shore looking at stuff in a whole new way. It was amazing. I can do this!"
>
> —novice kayaker Sally Lermond, after her first time in a sea kayak

COMMON CONCERNS

When you undertake a new sport, you will likely have questions you want answered and reassurances you need to hear before you begin. If you ignore these concerns, they can develop into stumbling blocks in your learning or thoughts that tinge your enjoyment with anxiety.

• •

"I overcome my fears by biting off just a smidgen more than I'm used to and gradually going on to more challenging stuff—not more dangerous, just more than I think my skill level will handle."

—Linda Legg,
kayak instructor and guide

• •

Following are some of the common concerns voiced by sea kayaking students.

Will I have trouble getting out of the boat if I turn over?

This can be a debilitating fear or just a mild concern that eases after your first capsize. Even a veteran kayaker like Judy Harrison had these fears as a beginner. "I felt pinned in a kayak," she remembers. "I felt very confined and vulnerable sitting inside a kayak with a spray cover on. I was used to kneeling in a canoe and feeling free to hop out." Now? "No problem!"

A sea kayaking class will take you through the steps of a wet exit. Unlike whitewater kayaks, most touring kayaks have roomy cockpits. They are simply not tight enough to hold a person hanging upside down—especially when you add the lubricant of water. Gravity is also in your favor, and the buoyancy in your PFD (personal flotation device) will bring you to the surface.

Wet exits are covered in detail in Chapter 5. If you have a disability that restricts your lower body mobility, you might be more comfortable in a boat with an oversized cockpit or in a sit-on-top model with no deck at all. Trust me when I tell you that once you've done a wet exit, you'll wonder why you thought it was such a big deal.

"COMMON CONCERNS"

• • • • • • • • • • • • • • • •

Overcoming fear

Time spent in your boat will do wonders to dispel fears and increase your confidence. Here are some comments from veteran kayakers about how they overcame some of their fears.

Linda Legg pushed her limits by challenging herself to try just a bit more than she was used to each time she went out. "I was drawn to this sport. I loved it, but things were scary. . . . When I got better in the surf, then the small waves weren't scary anymore—just the big ones were. When I started doing advanced training in tidal streams, the standing waves were as tall as two-story buildings. *That* was scary! I overcome my fears by biting off just a smidgen more than I'm used to and gradually going on to more challenging stuff—not more dangerous, just more than I think my skill level will handle."

When Joanne Turner started sea kayaking she was concerned about ocean swells and capsizing. She overcame her fears by paddling with a friend. "He had the same lack of skills and the same enthusiasm. We shared our first coastal trips, surf landing, and open-ocean crossings." They worked on

continued on page 24

continued from page 23

their skills together and explored the world by kayak. She and her paddling partner, Doug Schwartz, now instruct and run a kayaking business together.

My fear has always been a lack of stamina and managing fatigue. I have this notion that I will get halfway into a long crossing and not be able to finish. It hasn't ever happened, but it hovers in my mind, waiting to pounce every time I set out on open water. It makes me conservative in trip planning—I break every outing into small pieces that I can visualize. I reward myself for completing each of these small pieces and encourage myself to continue. If there are no immediate landmarks present, I imagine throwing a ball ahead of the boat, visualize where it will land, and paddle to that exact spot. When I get there, I visualize throwing the ball again, repeating the process until the worst is over. I often look up from retrieving my imaginary ball to realize I've reached my destination.

Whatever your concerns, think through them. Discuss them with other paddlers. Define what will ease your fears—practice, the presence of a sympathetic paddling partner, or detailed planning. Then go do it.

> "**I** felt pinned in a kayak. I felt very confined and vulnerable sitting inside a kayak with a spray cover on. I was used to kneeling in a canoe and feeling free to hop out." Now? "No problem!"
>
> —Judy Harrison, paddlesports advocate and publisher of *Canoe & Kayak Magazine*

Do I have to be really strong to do this?

Good technique and good planning are more important than physical strength. Understanding your own strengths and weaknesses in the planning stage makes a big difference.

Paddling utilizes many muscle groups—from the large muscles in the legs, torso, and abdomen, to the smaller muscles in your forearms. The best way to get these muscles in shape for paddling is to paddle! Stretching before and after paddling will help you stay loose and avoid soreness, especially when you first start out (see Chapter 9 for stretches for paddlers).

When you're on the water, the wind is usually your biggest tormentor. Think about how your boat reacts to wind and wave action. Too often, a novice paddler will waste a great deal of energy fighting the conditions and the characteristics of her boat rather than working within those factors to minimize their impact. Remember to plan plenty of rest and hydration stops out of the wind. Conserve your strength by using those paddling techniques you learned in your first class. In Chapter 7, I will give you some tips on paddling in the wind.

Will I get lost in open water or in fog?

Here, planning is everything. It is easy to get disoriented on open water or in the fog when landmarks are obscured or absent. When you plan a trip, try breaking it into several short segments. Each segment should start and end at an easily identifiable spot on your chart. This will provide you with a series of checkpoints at which you can decide whether to continue or retrace your path to return.

Basic navigation skills and the ability to read charts are essential if you are paddling on the ocean or on large lakes. Your chart will point out "road signs" such as buoys, lighthouses, and other navigational markers. A deck compass allows you to plot courses between these physical markers. And a watch helps you time your progress and fine-tune your course. Until you know how to use these tools correctly, you should paddle within sight of familiar land at all times. (Navigation is discussed in more detail in Chapter 8.)

My favorite time to paddle is in the fog. There is less boat traffic, the water is quieter, and the wildlife seems calmer. In the fog, it is easy to feel completely removed from the hustle and bustle of the mainland—even if you are only a few yards from shore. I was once paddling into a harbor that was thick with fog, and I heard the strangest sounds coming from what I judged to be the head of the harbor. Three bagpipers were playing on shore. I had the most magical experience as I slowly made my way in accompanied by this wonderful serenade.

Will I always need someone to help me when I go sea kayaking?

Many women are concerned that they will not be able to load and launch their boat without help. I was, and I still am. I've felt embarrassingly inadequate in some situations, but I muddled my way through them. So can you.

Some manufacturers have taken note of this problem. They market innovative pieces of equipment that help kayakers load their boats onto a vehicle by themselves. Some creativity and a piece or two of helpful equipment will solve the whole dilemma. (Tips on loading and carrying your boat are in Chapters 3 and 6.)

I don't want another sport with a lot of equipment maintenance!

Don't worry: Kayaking isn't one of them. There is little gear used in this sport that isn't durable and long lasting. Other than general cleanup and proper storage, sea kayakers don't have a demanding maintenance schedule.

Salt water, sand, and mud need to be flushed from your equipment. You should occasionally coat your boat with a good UV protectant to help maintain the color and delay UV degradation. This task is inexpensive and takes only a few minutes.

WE DID IT!

During a women's sea kayaking class, we were faced with loading a heavy boat on top of a van that none of us could reach from the ground. First, we nervously eyed the crowd for strong, tall specimens who could help us, and we made jokes about our situation. Then we got down to solving the problem.

Several women gathered flat stones and an old milk crate to position alongside the van as a step. Others emptied the boat to minimize its weight. We all grabbed the boat and carried it across the beach, over the hill, and into the parking lot. At the van, we passed the boat from the ground, to the first step, and to the top of the van, using spotters along the way. We did it! The next year I brought a kayak trolley, which made the carry a piece of cake, and two short ladders to use as steps.

• •

"This is not an easy sport. It requires judgment and stamina. But being way out from land in a little boat is a remarkable challenge, with limitless rewards for the prepared. Getting started? Find a good, fast boat. Then get a really good, light paddle. Always dress for the water temperature and always wear a PFD, which is the law. Find a mentor who can show you a few skills and who is competent in rescues. Learn to roll if you can. Finally, don't forget to go out at night when the August moon is full."

—Tamsin Venn, kayaking author and publisher of *Atlantic Coastal Kayaker*

• •

I have yet to be faced with any demanding maintenance tasks on a regular basis. To be honest, I rarely even wash out my gear. (But then, I am a serious abuser of gear and deserve all the jammed footbraces and corroded hardware I get!) The care and feeding of your equipment is discussed in Chapter 6.

Is seasickness very likely in a kayak?

No. I have seen it happen only twice, when the group was sitting still for a while in slow, rolling waves. If we'd started paddling sooner, I believe the problem would have been avoided. Novice paddlers will sometimes fixate on the bow of their boat instead of looking ahead, especially when they are tired or tense. This may lead to some queasiness in certain conditions. Remember to continue paddling. Look around you and ahead to the horizon line and you should be just fine. I am very prone to motion sickness, and I have only come close to feeling queasy in a kayak once. In that case, I had ignored all the tips I just gave you.

If you're not convinced you won't get seasick, try paddling in some gentle swells in an area with a nearby landing site to see how you feel. There are plenty of over-the-counter medications available for motion sickness, but you should be aware of the drowsiness or lack of balance that might result from their use.

Chapter 3

GETTING FRIENDLY WITH YOUR BOAT

Now you're ready to get into a boat. Don't worry if you don't have one yet: In the following section, I am going to give you a boat of your own. It will look a lot like the boat shown on the next page. You can choose its color (pick something bright so the boat will show up well on the water). It's important to get friendly with your boat. Be nosy. Pull off detachable covers and stick your head inside to look around. See how the seat feels. Kick your legs around in the cockpit. Roll your body like a rotisserie chicken. Sit in the seat like a cannonball. Think about how you could use this boat to get where you want to go.

NAMING OF THE PARTS

Before you do anything else with this imaginary boat, you need to learn the names of all its parts. Let's take a walking tour in and around the boat in the illustration on the next page.

The front of any boat is called the *bow*; the rear is called the *stern*. As you move toward the bow you are moving *forward*; as you move toward the stern you are moving *aft*. The top half of the kayak is the *deck*; the bottom half is the *hull*.

Your boat has an *overall length*, measured from tip to tip. It also has a *waterline length*, which is the length of the boat *in contact with the water*. Imagine putting your boat in scummy water. When

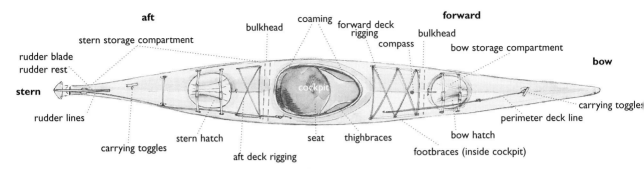

Become familiar with the names of all the parts and pieces of your sea kayak.

you lift it out, there is a ring around the boat. This scum line marks the waterline length. A boat's waterline length changes with loading, leaning, and even the density of the water. Overall length, on the other hand, never changes (unless you really crunch your boat!).

Continue to refer to the boat illustration above, and learn the following terms:

- **carrying toggles:** loops of webbing or little plastic handles at the bow and stern. You can lift your boat by the carrying toggles.

- **perimeter deck line:** line (or rope) running along the edges of the boat. The perimeter deck lines are handy for grabbing, especially if you're in the water. Rudder control lines often double as perimeter deck line on the stern.

- **bow storage compartment:** a storage space in the forward part of the boat; often called the bow hatch. The lids on storage compartments are called *hatch covers.*

- **bulkhead:** a watertight wall that separates storage compartments from the cockpit. Most sea kayaks have a bow bulkhead and a stern bulkhead. Some models have a third bulkhead to create a small day hatch accessible from the cockpit.

- **compass:** the small navigation aid we're all familiar with; in this case it's mounted somewhere on the forward deck. The deck-mounted compass functions the same way as a handheld compass but is designed to be read at a glance while you're paddling. Deck compasses may be permanently mounted or clipped across deck rigging for easy removal.

- **forward deck rigging:** pieces of bungee cord that cross the forward deck; used to secure items such as charts, water bottle, or safety gear.

- **cockpit:** the space in which the paddler sits.

- **footbraces:** pedals inside the cockpit on which you rest your feet while paddling.

Footbraces often double as rudder control pedals. They push along sliding tracks and are adjustable for leg length.

- **thighbraces:** contoured sections at the forward end of the cockpit opening that help fit the boat to your upper legs, providing better boat control. Thighbraces are often custom-padded with foam to fit your body shape; thus, when you move your knee or upper leg, the kayak moves with it.

- **coaming:** the edge around the cockpit opening. The lip shape of the coaming provides a place to attach the sprayskirt.

- **seat:** where the paddler sits. Seats usually are tilted for comfort and provide back support with a padded band or solid seatback. Seat bases are not movable, but seat backs usually are adjustable.

- **rudder lines:** lines that control the lifting and dropping of the rudder blade. There are numerous kinds of rudder lines. They should be easy to operate from a seated position in the cockpit.

- **aft deck rigging:** pieces of bungee cord that cross the aft deck; used to secure items such as safety gear, a spare paddle, or camping supplies.

- **stern storage compartment:** a storage compartment in the aft portion of the boat. Stern storage compartment usually have larger openings than bow compartments, because the stern deck is usually broader and flatter than the bow deck.

- **rudder:** a flat blade that can be dropped into the water at the stern and controlled by foot pedals in the cockpit. The ***rudder system*** provides directional stability in certain conditions. When not in use, the rudder blade rests on the stern deck, usually held in place by a ***rudder rest.***

GETTING ADJUSTED

Before putting a boat into the water, get comfortable sitting in the cockpit and make the adjustments necessary for a proper fit. Your boat should provide sufficient back support so you can maintain good posture in a seated position for several hours without feeling lower back fatigue. Seat backs are either fixed or adjustable; if you can, bring yours forward to give yourself solid support. No part of the seat or the cockpit rim (the coaming) should rub or gouge you uncomfortably.

Your boat should have some type of footbrace or footrest. You can adjust this for your leg length so your feet rest against something solid.

Before adjusting your footbraces, bring your heels in toward the center of the boat and let your knees fall out so your lower body forms a diamond shape (see illustration on page 30). This is the position you will use for paddling throughout the day. In all but the largest cockpits, your knees should fit comfortably under the outer edges of the cockpit so you can rock the boat back and forth by lifting your knee on either side. With the balls of your feet resting on the footbraces, you can also maintain this diamond-shaped position and be able to push against the footrests to securely hold yourself in the boat.

You may choose to customize the fit of your own boat by using foam padding in various spots. You can carve blocks of closed-cell foam and glue them into your boat to make the boat fit more snugly, provide additional back support, and cushion points where you continually rub against the boat (such as the area under your heels). This process of customizing your boat is discussed in detail in Chapter 6.

With your seatback and footbraces properly adjusted, you are ready to put your boat in the water.

CARRYING YOUR BOAT

The easiest way to carry a sea kayak is to have a person on either end. Most boats have carrying toggles, which make it easy to hold the boat as you walk. Many paddlers find it more comfortable and secure to carry the boat by cupping the end of the boat with their hands and then resting it against their hip as they walk. If you are carrying a heavily loaded boat, you should always hold your hand underneath, in addition to using the toggles.

If you prefer to carry the boat by yourself, you can either use a cart or carry the boat on your shoulder.

Your lower body must be in contact with your kayak for solid boat control. With your knees out and your heels in, your lower body forms a diamond shape.

Two people carry a kayak more easily than one. Grip the carrying toggles and cup your hand under the hull for backup support and balance.

A kayak cart that slides on from the stern is easy to use. It folds up for stowing in the rear hatch.

Center carts balance heavier loads and can be used on a wider range of kayak models.

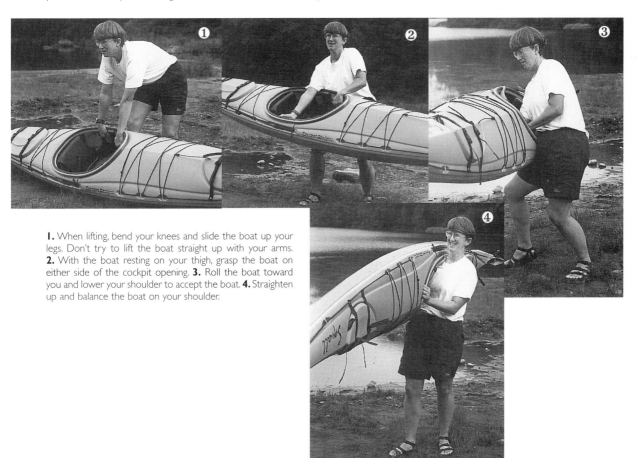

1. When lifting, bend your knees and slide the boat up your legs. Don't try to lift the boat straight up with your arms. **2.** With the boat resting on your thigh, grasp the boat on either side of the cockpit opening. **3.** Roll the boat toward you and lower your shoulder to accept the boat. **4.** Straighten up and balance the boat on your shoulder.

Using a kayak cart or trolley is my favorite way to carry a boat. Carts come in a variety of designs. Not only do they allow you to transport your boat by yourself; you can also load the kayak full of your gear to make a single trip to the water. Some models even fold up to fit into a hatch, so you can take the cart with you.

Use the following steps to carry your kayak on your shoulder. Don't try to bend over and lift the boat up to your shoulder: You might strain your lower back. These steps are designed to help you avoid back strain.

"**U**se an upside down bucket or one or two ladders and experiment with ways of lifting your kayak on and off your vehicle. There are lots of possibilities. I am 4'10" and can do it, so almost everyone else can, too. If you can't, acknowledge that and bring a friend along or get comfortable asking strangers at your launch site to help you. No problem."

—veteran instructor Joanne Turner

- Bend your knees slightly and slide the boat up your leg by grabbing it with both hands inside the cockpit rim.

- Rest the boat on your thigh; then roll the cockpit toward you until you can begin to get your shoulder inside of it.

- Shift the weight of the boat from your thigh to your shoulder. Use your arms to steady the boat as you straighten your legs.

- As the boat rests on your shoulder, find its balance point to make the carry easier. (Some paddlers find it difficult to carry a boat this way since it can be unwieldy to balance longer models—especially on a windy day.) If the coaming cuts into your shoulder, use a life vest for padding.

GETTING YOUR BOAT ON AND OFF A VEHICLE

The subject women sea kayakers voice the most frustration about is getting their boats on and off their cars. And with good reason. The combination of tall vehicles and small people can definitely lead to some head scratching.

When solo loading, work with one end of the boat at a time. Put the stern up first or make sure to protect it from the ground. You don't want to grind dirt and gravel into the rudder when you lift the bow. If your vehicle is too tall for you to place the stern onto the rack, step onto a bucket or short stepladder. Do the same when you lift the bow.

You may be placing your boat into a set of foam cradles or into cradles that are part of a

Side loading: Protect the stern and then lift the bow into the cradles. You may need a stepladder or bucket.

Lift the stern and push the boat forward until it is balanced on the cradles. Yakima's Hully-Rollers or cloth-lined cradles make this easier.

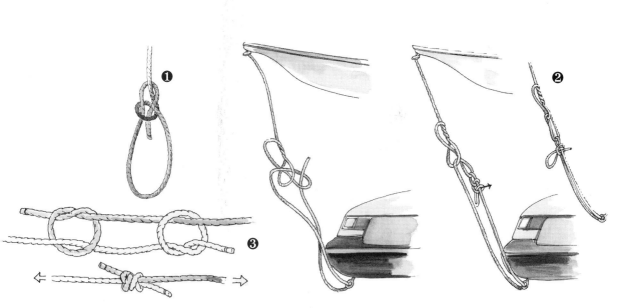

1. The useful bowline knot gives you a bombproof loop in the end of a line but is easy to undo. **2.** Use a trucker's hitch to secure the bow and stern of your kayak to the car. Having a line off the bow and the stern holds the boat steady in strong crosswinds and is a good backup to your roof-rack attachment points. **3.** A fisherman's knot joins two ends of the same line together to form a loop. Double or triple these knots for added insurance. You'll use this knot to make your rescue sling (see pages 64–65).

complete car rack system. When you set the boat in place, make sure you temporarily secure the boat to the top of your car. Strong crosswinds can easily peel your boat from the roof of your car before you get everything attached. To secure the boat for travel, tighten down the straps until they are snug. Then tie a bow and stern line to your bumper or bumper hooks. Page 33 shows some helpful knots.

Be careful not to overtighten any straps or lines. You should never see the boat flex or flatten. Try to position the straps outside of the coaming and, if possible, where the bulkheads are positioned. Your rack system and the style of your car may dictate strap placement. If the boat has a rudder, secure it in place.

Another method for solo loading involves working from the rear of the vehicle. (If the car is really tall or the rack is far forward, this method doesn't work very well.) Place the bow onto the car's rear rack or roof edge. You may want to temporarily cushion the car with a piece of carpet. Since the stern is on the ground, throw a life vest or some sort of padding under it to protect the rudder. Once the bow is on the rear rack or roof edge, pick up the stern and slide the boat forward until it is in place. If you are using cradles, you may need to line them with short-nap carpet or stretch a piece of pantyhose over them so the boat will slide easily. If needed, you can use a short step at the rear of the vehicle. Secure the boat as outlined above.

❶ **Loading from the rear:** Protect the stern and place the bow in the rear cradle. A towel or piece of carpet will help to protect your vehicle.

Lift the stern and push forward until it is balanced on the cradles. ❷

❸ Cinch-down straps make it easy to secure your kayak. Cinch the straps snugly but don't overtighten.

In case you haven't figured it out, loaded boats should always be pointed with the bow forward. To do otherwise will bring bad karma to you and your boat! All self-respecting kayakers know this fact and would never question its validity.

Play around with different methods of loading and make one work for you. Manufacturers are finally offering tools for loading boats. Given the positive response in the marketplace, I would expect that other equipment will be developed over the next few years. There are now at least three pieces of gear available that help with solo loading or with the combination of short people and tall vehicles. Two of them, Voyageur's Overloader and Thule's Outrigger, provide you with a place to park one end of your boat before lifting the other end onto your rack. The third, Yakima's HullyRollers, provides a set of rollers that cradle the boat and can be pivoted. The boat can be rolled across the cradles and into place. These cradles are then locked into position before driving away.

Whichever way you approach loading, don't let it intimidate you or prevent you from going paddling. Store your boat on racks outside (out of direct sunlight) or on racks or slings in a garage that are easy to access. With a little creative thinking, you will feel free to grab your boat and go whenever you want.

GETTING IN AND OUT

It can be a tricky proposition to get in and out of your boat at the water's edge—at least gracefully! It is not uncommon to see a sleek, stylish kayak repeatedly dump its passenger like a nautical bucking bronco.

Getting in and out of your boat is a matter of balance and support. You must create a support system that anchors all the components to one another: the paddler, the boat, the paddle, and the shoreline. If there is no shoreline in a convenient location, you may need to support yourself on a dock, a ladder, or another boat. Some agile paddlers might straddle the boat from behind the seat and slip easily in and out. But under most circumstances, you will need more support.

When entering your boat, your weight is supported by the extended paddle as you slip your feet into the cockpit.

After your feet are in the boat, drop your hips into the seat. To exit the boat, reverse the process: hips first, feet last.

When entering or exiting your boat in calm water, pull parallel to the shoreline or low dock. Place your paddle behind your cockpit coaming. The paddle should be positioned perpendicular to your kayak, and it should extend out so it rests on something solid, such as the shore or dock. This way, your paddle acts like a fixed arm that stabilizes your boat.

With one hand, grasp the paddle shaft and the cockpit coaming tightly. Slide your other hand down the paddle shaft about 3 feet. With this support system you can slide in and out of your cockpit. The boat will not swing away from you because it is anchored to the shoreline with your paddle. With your weight supported in this boat/paddle/shore system, you can move your feet in and out of the cockpit. Enter with your feet (one at a time) leading the way. Exit with your butt leading the way. Always support your weight and keep your balance using your paddle.

To make this work, several things must occur more or less simultaneously:

- Your paddle must remain perpendicular to your kayak, be fully extended, and be held firmly to the boat for maximum support.

- You must enter or exit your boat from the supported side only.

- One end of your extended paddle must rest on your boat, and the other end must rest on something solid (*e.g.*, the shore or dock).

- Keep your center of gravity low and keep your weight only on the side supported by your paddle.

Ignoring any of these steps will turn a graceful move into an embarrassing spill.

When you are entering or exiting your boat in surf, you need to move quickly to avoid taking on water or having the boat taken from you by the surge. Using the same steps described earlier, get into your boat in just enough water to float it (it will be even easier with very little water under your boat). Keep your boat perpendicular to the waves. This way, you won't get washed back up on the beach and turned sideways. Never allow yourself to get caught between your boat and the beach in surf. You might get clipped by your boat if it is lifted and thrown toward the shore by a wave.

Once you've entered your boat, you can "walk" it to the water using your hands or your paddle as a push pole. When the water is deep enough, begin paddling.

• •

"The first time I sat in a kayak I honestly thought I'd tip right over if I even blinked my eyes. Thank goodness I was wrong! My instructor told me to relax and got me to swing my hips back and forth and the boat with them. After that I never felt like the boat was going to dump me out. I felt like I was in control."

—new kayaker Lynne Mahoney

• •

Entering and exiting your boat alongside a high dock is a real challenge. When exiting, if the top of the dock is reachable from your boat, try to transfer your weight from the boat as you chin-up to the dock, hoist yourself up on your elbows, and then swing your butt up onto the dock. Keep your feet (but very little weight) in your boat. When entering the kayak from the dock, slowly lower yourself, feet first, from the dock edge into the cockpit. You won't be able to use your paddle as a support when you transfer your weight to and from the dock.

If you are alongside a pier with a long drop to the water, you may be forced to use a pier ladder rung as part of your support system. Again, the trick is to slowly transfer your weight away from your cockpit and onto the ladder. As long as you are firmly anchored to the ladder, the boat should remain in place and be a reasonably stable platform. Once you are out of the boat, you can attach a line to the ladder to temporarily hold the boat.

When you go kayaking, the first skill a casual observer sees is how confidently you enter or exit your boat—so it's worth smoothing out the rough spots to make this move as graceful as possible. Even if your vanity doesn't demand this, a proper entrance will keep you from getting wet before you even start your trip!

BALANCE AND THE ART OF STAYING UPRIGHT

A great deal of your boat control comes from your lower body. You can change your boat's hull configuration by leaning the boat on edge during a tight turn. You can right a boat that has begun to turn over by swinging your hips and bringing the boat back under you. Remember to stay loose in the hips to maintain your balance. You can shift your weight in the cockpit to help trim the boat as you maintain a particular course. It is important that your boat fit properly: A sloppy fit will make it difficult for you to lean your boat. You'll end up sliding to the lower side of your seat each time you lift one edge. Make sure your footbraces and seat are properly adjusted, and refer to "Customizing Your Boat" in Chapter 6 (pages 88–89) for more information on fit.

Your boat can handle sizable seas and rough water if you let it. But first, you must learn to relax. Paddlers get into trouble in rough water when they stiffen up and don't allow their bodies to move fluidly with the motion of the boat. Think of your torso and your lower body as being connected by a swivel joint that allows you to rotate and swing freely at the hips. Now, when the boat begins to tip in a direction you want to avoid, simply swing your hip on the downward side back up to bring the boat level again.

Practicing **J**-leans with a spotter helps you find the balance points in your boat and enhances your flexibility and strength.

• •

*"**L**oose hips save ships"*

—an old kayaking adage!

• •

Using **J**-leans is a good way to work on your balance and discover more about your boat's stability. To do this, you form a **J** with your body by bringing one side of the boat up with your hip. This will lower the other side of the boat, even to the point of water entering the cockpit. With the boat on edge, it is important to keep your torso upright and over the center of your boat's buoyancy. This point shifts from the center of the cockpit to the shoulder of the boat as you lean the boat on edge. If you lean away from your boat's buoyancy, you will capsize without the support of your paddle (more on this in the next chapter).

The key to balancing in a **J**-lean is to stay loose and keep your weight centered and still. When you start practicing **J**-leans, have someone spot you in shallow water by standing close to your boat. This person will be your additional support until you feel comfortable doing **J**-leans on your own.

As you practice **J**-leans on both sides, try to bring the boat edge higher each time. You will find that maintaining a **J**-lean will require strength in your thighs, abdomen, and hips. You can build these muscles by holding a **J**-lean for an extended period. Use a dock or pool edge for handy support until you are completely comfortable with this technique.

As you get confident in your **J**-lean, you will find your boat's balance points and learn to maintain your balance. This will be valuable when the boat rocks beneath you in rough water or when you lean your boat during a turning stroke. (See Chapter 4 for a discussion of turning strokes.)

Being confident in using your lower body to control your boat will enhance all your paddling skills and let you relax on the water.

Your dream boat does exist, somewhere. Right now, your ideal may be just a flicker of an idea. Or it might be a specific model that is sending its siren song out to you from the window of your local paddling shop.

As you search for your dream boat, you'll be faced with a myriad of choices. You will find kayaks that are short and fat, long and sleek, and everything in between. There will be 18-foot boats that weigh less than 40 pounds and 8-foot boats that weigh more than 40 pounds.

Choosing the right boat for you might seem overwhelming at this point. Don't worry. In Chapter 6, you will learn about boats and gear in great detail. Right now, the main thing is to get in a boat. Keeping in mind the terms defined in this chapter, get in lots of boats. Try a sea kayak tour. Sign up for your first sea kayaking class. You will begin to understand what each boat is trying to tell you. Then, go try some more boats.

Somewhere along the line you will get into a boat and, like Goldilocks, you'll know it is "just right." If you have good self-control, you'll be able to hold off purchasing a boat until you understand what type is best for you. In the meantime, develop your idea of your dream boat. Think how good it will look on the water with you in it!

Chapter 4

PADDLE STROKES AND CONTROLLING YOUR BOAT

Up until this point, I have all but ignored an essential piece of equipment: your paddle. As a novice, you will have a love-hate relationship with your paddle. You will blame it for fatigue, curse it when your boat goes off course, and even distrust it at times. Yet, you will be totally dependent on your paddle. It will get you where you want to go. On a good day, it will be a seamless extension of your body.

GETTING TO KNOW YOUR PADDLE

Before you take a single stroke, you need to learn some basics about this essential piece of equipment.

The anatomy of your paddle

Kayak paddles have two blades, one at either end of the shaft. This very smart and practical leap in paddle design occurred sometime in the ancient history of kayaking. Having a blade on either end of the paddle means you always have a blade ready to go to work for you on either side. This minimizes your motion and effort and allows you to easily find and maintain a paddling cadence over the miles. And unlike when paddling a tandem canoe, you'll never be stuck paddling opposite your partner's favorite side.

Your paddle blades have two surfaces: the powerface and the backface. *Powerface* refers to the working face of the blade during your forward stroke. *Backface* refers to the back of the blade during the forward stroke. It is important to remember the difference between the two, since strokes may be described as using the powerface or the backface. The powerface is always the powerface, regardless of which stroke you are using. If your paddle has spooned blades, the powerface is the concave side, and the backface is the convex side.

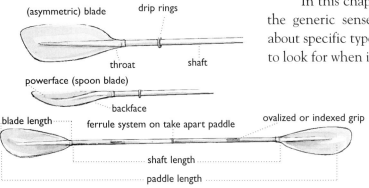

A typical touring kayak paddle has asymmetric blades that are spoon-shaped. Most models can be taken apart for easy storage.

In this chapter we will talk about paddles in the generic sense. In Chapter 6 you will learn about specific types of paddles so you'll know what to look for when it comes time to make equipment buying decisions.

A proper grip

When you hold your paddle, don't use a white-knuckle grip. That can cause forearm cramps and wrist injuries and wastes your energy. Relax.

To properly space the placement of your hands, hold the paddle up to your shoulders with the shaft centered on your chest. For a comfortable grip, your hands should be placed on the shaft just outside of your shoulders.

Check your hands every now and then to make sure they haven't traveled down the shaft and are no longer equidistant from the center. If your hands are not equidistant from the center, your forward stroke will be out of kilter and it will be more difficult to go straight. If your hands are too close to the center, you lose the ability to use torso rotation (see "Forward stroke" on page 42 for explanation of torso rotation). If your hands are too far apart, you'll find yourself leaning forward to reach the water, which will be awkward.

Keep your hands a little more than shoulder-width apart for a comfortable and efficient grip. Keep the paddle centered on your chest.

Make sure you are holding your paddle so the powerface is the blade face you are working during your forward stroke. Most manufacturers display their name and logo on the blades' surfaces. If you orient the blades so this is readable, you've probably got it right! If your paddle has asymmetric blades (one side of the blade slightly longer than the other), position the blade so the longer portion is at the top. This orientation maximizes the efficiency of this blade design.

For times when you need a quick support stroke or are setting up for a roll, it is important to know exactly how to orient your paddle without looking at it. Most paddles' grip areas are not round like the rest of the paddle shaft, but rather are oval in shape. This is more comfortable to grip, and it helps you quickly orient the paddle. Don't flip the paddle around in your hands so you lose track of its orientation—this bad habit will come back to haunt you.

Orient an asymmetric blade so the longer portion of the blade is at the top and the concave surface is facing you.

PADDLE STROKES

There are paddle strokes that will power your boat over long distances, serve as a set of brakes, or turn or move your boat sideways. Each stroke combines paddle, boat, and your body orientation in ways to maximize its effectiveness.

When you practice paddle strokes, stay relaxed and let the stroke develop and become fluid. At first you'll probably think too much about each movement. But by repeating and refining

TO FEATHER OR NOT TO FEATHER

On your first day in a kayak, you may be asked to make a choice you are not yet prepared to make: whether to use a feathered or unfeathered paddle.

The difference between feathered and unfeathered paddles is how the two paddle blades are positioned in relation to each other. On an unfeathered paddle, both paddle blades are in the same plane. On a feathered paddle, one blade is set at an angle to the other. This angle is usually between 60 and 90 degrees.

When using an unfeathered paddle, your hands remain in the same position and orientation on the shaft throughout your forward stroke. With a feathered paddle, one hand (called the control hand) remains fixed; the paddle shaft is allowed to rotate in your other (noncontrol) hand in order to set up for the stroke on that side.

continued on page 42

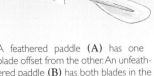

A feathered paddle (**A**) has one blade offset from the other. An unfeathered paddle (**B**) has both blades in the same plane.

continued from page 41

Kayak instructors can spend hours arguing about blade angles, wrist torques, and other esoteric subjects. As a novice, you just want to get going! If you can, try both feathered and unfeathered paddles. Test paddles with different feather angle settings. Then choose the paddle and feather angle you like best. In the end, what's important is that you become comfortable with the style you choose and polish your technique. Don't switch back and forth: You may lose your instinctive knowledge of blade orientation.

Be sure to keep your wrist straight when you paddle. Avoid bending it side to side, which can result in injury. If you keep the back of your hand and your forearm aligned, you will be fine. Maintaining a loose grip, keeping your wrists straight, and using a good paddling technique will prevent you from having a problem with your wrists—regardless of your choice of feather angle.

I believe good technique and feathered paddles have a symbiotic relationship and that feather angles in the 60- to 75-degree range are less stressful to the wrist. Of course, I'm one of those instructors who enjoys arguing for hours about esoteric subjects!

each stroke, you will help your muscles capture a memory of each movement. Over time all these movements will become smooth and flow naturally. Every time you get in a boat, consider running through your stroke repertoire as a warm-up. Let each stroke flow into another as you create your own sequence—your own ballet.

Every paddle stroke contains three distinct phases: catch, propulsion, and recovery. The *catch* is defined by the particular placement of the blade in the water and its angle at the beginning of the stroke. The *propulsion* phase is defined by the movement of the blade through the water in a particular fashion. The *recovery* phase is defined by how the blade is returned to its position for the next stroke.

Forward stroke

Your forward stroke is the engine that drives your boat, and you will repeat this movement thousands of times during a day's paddle. Take time to develop an efficient touring stroke that you can use to click off the miles. It will be well worth the effort.

If you ignore the foundation of good technique for your forward stroke, you doom yourself to a slogging, graceless style that is hard work. With an efficient technique, you will be able to paddle longer and work less. In the beginning, you may feel somewhat awkward. But after a few sessions, your forward stroke should feel graceful and intuitive.

• •

"You never realize how important a forward stroke is until yours gets really good, and then you always want to refine it and tune it. It's a stroke I try to work on every time I get in a boat!"

—Deb Shapiro, co-owner of The Kayak Centre

• •

The power of your forward stroke comes primarily from your torso rotation, not from your arms. With your arms, you can only draw on the short muscles of the fore- and upper arm. With your torso, you can utilize the long, powerful muscles of the back and abdomen. Torso rotation is the great equalizer for touring paddlers. Over the long haul, technique overshadows muscle mass and raw power every time.

Your forward stroke starts from the ball of your foot as it pushes gently against the footbrace on the side you are paddling on. Your torso then winds up, and you lead with your shoulder as you place the paddle blade in the water. Your blade enters the water at a point about even with your shin. Rather than pulling back with your arms, let your torso unwind and drive your upper hand forward. Your boat moves through the water, and you begin to set your blade up on the other side. If you had a bell attached to your belly button, it would ring with each stroke as you rotate your torso from side to side.

1. Make the catch of the forward stroke alongside your shin. Note that there is little bend in either elbow. **2.** Keep the top hand relaxed as it pushes through the stroke. The paddle shaft remains parallel to the torso throughout the stroke. **3.** The propulsion phase is complete when the blade is alongside your hip. **4.** The recovery phase sets up the other blade to enter the water. The boat should remain flat in the water as it moves forward.

Monitor the following things as you learn the forward stroke.

- **Elbows.** Your elbows should be bent only slightly throughout the stroke, which keeps the paddle shaft out in front and squared with your torso. Don't pump your arms like a bicycle rider's legs. Imagine that something really smelly is on the paddle shaft and you want to keep it well away from you.

- **Posture.** Don't lean forward or slouch in your seat during the forward stroke. This will limit your torso rotation.

- **Upper hand.** Your upper hand should not cross the centerline of the boat during the forward stroke. For a relaxed touring stroke, it should remain at shoulder level or below. If you lose sight of it, it's too high. Your upper hand should be relaxed as it pushes the paddle through the stroke.

- **Wrist.** Your wrist should not bend back and forth or from side to side with each stroke. Keep your wrist straight and your hand relaxed. The back of your hand should be in line with your forearm.

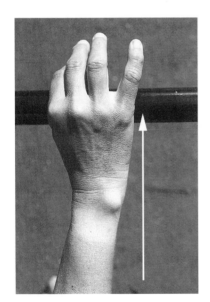

During your forward stroke, the back of your hand, wrist, and forearm should all be aligned. Avoid any side-to-side movement of the wrist.

Your forward stroke should be made close to the side of your boat and should come out of the water next to your hip. Trailing the paddle behind you slows your forward momentum and might even send you off course. Try to establish an easy cadence that you can maintain for at least an hour. A steady pace you can maintain easily is far better than a quick start followed by an erratic rhythm. Your boat should remain flat and calm in the water. There shouldn't be any sudden jerks or yanks in your forward stroke that cause your boat to bounce or rock. That type of movement wastes energy.

Back stroke

The back stroke is sometimes the forgotten stroke. Novice paddlers often raise their paddles out of the water and hope their boat stops. A quick series of back strokes serves as a set of brakes. There are also definite advantages to making a quick move in reverse.

Your back stroke uses the backface of the paddle blade. Don't flip your paddle over and use the powerface from your forward stroke.

You can use torso rotation to drive your back stroke the same way you did with your forward stroke. Since you are reaching behind you, look back as you plant your blade. This helps you rotate your torso. It also helps you avoid catching the paddle blade under the boat and causing a capsize. You may want to angle your paddle so the backface of the blade is tilted toward the water. This will give you more support during the stroke, since you'll have more of your blade's surface area pushing down on the water.

1. Always look at the paddle blade as you begin your backstroke. The paddle shaft is parallel to the torso. **2.** For additional support, flatten the paddle blade slightly as it moves through the stroke. **3.** As you begin to set up for the catch on the other side, your torso must rotate.

Turning (sweep) strokes

Most touring kayaks are designed for efficient travel, where tracking in a straight line is more important than the ability to turn quickly. In all but the shortest boats, a quick turn requires an understanding of boat dynamics and the confidence to lean your boat and reach out away from it.

Imagine leaning your 17-foot-long sea kayak on its side (or shoulder). When you do this, you shorten the waterline length dramatically as both ends of the boat come out of the water. You have now transformed your long, straight-tracking boat into a short, maneuverable boat. Changing the hull configuration by leaning your boat is a useful technique. Remember, leaning your boat does not mean leaning your body. It means leaning the boat while keeping your body over the boat's buoyant shoulder in a **J**-lean. (Review "Balance and the art of staying upright" in Chapter 3.)

1. A kayak sitting calmly in flat water has a maximum waterline length. A long waterline length is more efficient and tracks straighter.
2. Lean the boat to increase the maneuverability of a kayak of a given waterline length. This shortens the waterline length by getting both ends out of the water.

Now that you know how to shorten your boat length for a turn, you are ready to do a sweep stroke. A forward sweep stroke begins with your paddle blade in the water, about even with your foot. Using the powerface of the blade, make a sweeping motion in a long arc out and away from the boat and back in to the stern. You should lean your boat toward the side of the stroke. Your boat will turn away from the stroke. For example, if you are making a forward sweep stroke on the right side and leaning to your right, your boat will swing to the left.

Following are a few tips.

- **Always look at your paddle blade throughout a sweep stroke.** This will allow you to monitor the blade's orientation to the water and enable you to make adjustments to maximize support when needed. You can also make sure the blade is pulled out of the water before it ends up under the boat and causes a capsize.

- **Use the powerface for extra support.** Tilt the powerface of the blade toward the water for some extra support during the forward sweep stroke. If your lean is a little shaky, your blade face will help you.

- **Use the full range of the stroke.** The latter half of the sweep stroke is the most powerful, since the stern is freer to swing in response to the stroke. Take advan-

1. The catch of the sweep stroke is made alongside your foot. Begin to lean your boat toward the side of the stroke. **2.** Keep your eyes on the paddle blade as it sweeps through the water. The paddle shaft is parallel to the torso. **3.** The latter part of the sweep stroke is the most powerful but requires the most flexibility. **4.** As you finish the sweep stroke, lift the paddle blade out of the water so the boat doesn't trip over it and capsize.

tage of this by utilizing the full range of the stroke. Make sure to mirror the blade's movement with your torso and keep your eyes on the blade.

- **Tilt the backface of the blade so it is parallel to the water during the recovery phase.** If you need to make more than one sweep stroke, it is most efficient to keep leaning your boat over during the recovery phase. However, leaning your boat when there is no support from your paddle is dicey. After you remove your blade from the water, cock the blade so the backface is parallel to the water and just above the water's surface. If your lean becomes shaky during the recovery phase, you will have a blade face ready for quick support. (See "Support strokes," pages 49–52.)

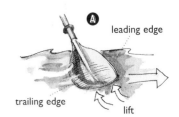

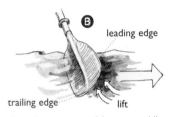

To gain support and keep a paddle blade from diving, lift the leading edge of the blade slightly, using either the powerface **(A)** or the backface **(B)**.

The sweep stroke sounds complicated only because you are introducing several new techniques. The stroke itself is simple: Make a forward stroke in a sweeping pattern on one side of your boat and your boat will turn the other way. By adding a boat lean, you make the stroke more powerful and graceful. By adding blade angle subtleties, you ensure support throughout all phases of the stroke. When you practice your sweep strokes, begin with your boat flat in the water. Gradually add the techniques that will make the stroke more powerful, graceful, and supportive.

A reverse sweep is simply a sweep stroke that starts from the back of the boat (the stern) and moves toward the front (the bow). Everything with the reverse sweep stroke is simply reversed. The reverse sweep stroke uses the backface of the blade and starts at the stern, while the forward sweep stroke uses the powerface of the blade and starts at the bow. A reverse sweep done

1. Look back to the catch of the blade as you begin your reverse sweep stroke. **2.** To make the stroke more powerful, lean the boat toward it. The paddle shaft is parallel to the torso throughout the stroke. **3.** As your torso rotates, the blade is driven through the water and exits the water alongside your foot.

on the right side of your boat turns your boat toward the right; a reverse sweep stroke on the left side of your boat turns your boat toward the left.

You can enhance the reverse sweep stroke the same way you enhanced the forward sweep stroke: by shortening your boat's waterline length with a lean and using your blade angle for support. The reverse sweep stroke is a powerful and supportive stroke because you can lean on the backface of the blade if you need to.

By combining a forward sweep stroke on one side with a reverse sweep stroke on the other side, you can turn your boat with a minimum number of strokes. But this combination will stop all forward momentum. This combination is useful when you need to turn your boat around in restricted quarters, such as a boat slip or launching area, or when you need a decisive reversal of direction.

When should you use the forward sweep and when should you use the reverse sweep? Use a forward sweep stroke when you want to maintain forward motion and when you need the powerful combination of a forward sweep and a reverse sweep for a complete turnaround. Use a reverse sweep stroke when you want to turn and look behind you and when you want to turn and stop your forward momentum.

Support strokes

You learned the usefulness of having your paddle blade for support with sweep strokes. If you ever did a belly flop off a diving board, you learned that water has surprising resistance when slapped with a fairly flat object—like your unfortunate belly! You can use your paddle blade the same way by slapping the water to gain a quick bit of support. These support strokes are called *braces,* and they come in a variety of fashions: slap (low and high) and sculling (low and high).

Naming a brace low or high is based on whether you use the powerface or the backface of the blade for support. If you use the powerface, you are doing a high brace. Your wrists roll back and your knuckles point up so the powerface is parallel to the water. If you use the backface, you are doing a low brace. Your wrists roll forward and your knuckles point down so the backface is parallel to the water. You can do a low or a high brace on either side of your boat. The top two photos on page 50 demonstrate a low brace; the bottom two show a high brace.

Imagine that you are starting to tip over in your boat. You have two tools that will prevent a capsize: your balance and your paddle. If you use these two tools simultaneously, you will maximize their effectiveness.

A brace should always work in concert with your lower body. While you are slapping or stirring the water with your paddle blade to gain support, your lower body should be bringing the boat back to a more stable position underneath you.

A slap brace is a short-lived move. It buys you just enough time to snap the boat back up quickly. A sculling brace allows you more leisure in regaining your balance (and since they look cool, they are usually seen at launch sites where people feel the need to show off their skills).

1. The low brace uses the backface of the paddle blade for support. Hold the paddle shaft parallel to the torso and low to the boat. **2.** The low brace is short-lived but powerful for a quick righting of the boat. **3.** The high brace uses the powerface of the blade. Hold the shaft close and parallel to the torso. **4.** The elbows remain low and close to the body. This protects the shoulder throughout the high brace, even in moving water.

Slap brace

Slap the water with your paddle blade while you lift your lower hip to bring the boat up underneath you. Once you slap the water with your paddle blade you must remove it quickly. Otherwise, it will begin to dive and you will pull yourself over trying to remove it from the water's grip. Your slap should be immediately followed by a quick roll of your wrists, which slices the blade out of the water. This quick roll of your wrists makes removal from the water easier: You are turning the blade edge up and away from the water rather than trying to lift the entire blade straight up and lifting water as well.

Practice this move while sitting flat in your boat, using both high and low brace positions. Feel the difference in resistance—first as you press down and then as you try to remove the blade from the water.

Sculling brace

When you do a sculling brace, you keep your paddle moving in the water and use this movement for support. Your support in a sculling brace is more than momentary. It will continue as long as you move the paddle often enough and in the correct orientation.

Think of making horizontal, elongated figure eights on top of or slightly below the surface of the water with your paddle. Your sculling motion should be at least 3 feet from one end to the other. A shorter range of movement is less supportive.

This movement will give you continuous support as long as your paddle does not dive and take you with it. To avoid having your paddle dive, remember to keep the leading edge of your paddle blade up to gain lift—if you don't it will tend to be pushed down as it moves forward through the water. Spoon blade designs will accentuate this tendency. Your leading edge will change depending on the direction of your moving blade during your figure eights.

As you gain confidence in your sculling brace, lean your boat over farther and farther. As long as you keep your paddle moving, you should be able to support yourself on this sculling brace. When you are ready to quit, lift your hip and knee (try your head dink here) to bring the boat back up under you as you continue to scull. Use your lower body to bring the boat under you rather than pressing on your paddle to sit back upright.

THE HEAD DINK

To help free your hips for a quick and fluid lift to bring the boat back under you, try dropping your head toward the lower side of the boat. This move is called a *head dink*. It may seem unnatural to drop your head toward the water. But when you do, your hip is easier to lift, and it brings the boat with it. Try your J-lean first using a head dink and then without a head dink. See if you can feel a difference.

Drop your head toward the water to free your hips to snap the boat back up underneath you. This move is called a head dink.

A sculling brace buys you time and support. Move the paddle in elongated figure eights with the leading edge of the blade providing lift.

PEANUT BUTTER SANDWICHES

• • • • • • • • • • • • • • • • • • • •

Visualize (or actually do this if you're hungry) making a peanut butter sandwich with big globs of peanut butter on your knife. As you spread the peanut butter on the bread (imagine very soft white bread for the sake of argument), you must slightly lift the leading edge of the knife as you push forward or it will bury itself in the glob and tear the bread. As you move the knife back through the other side of your figure eight, you must lift that leading edge as well. You've just done a sculling brace on your peanut butter sandwich. Now, eat up and try it in your boat!

Most paddlers flail their sculling braces on the surface of the water, which creates a lot of foam and noise. Water is denser than foam, and it offers more support for a brace. Paddle movement below the surface is actually more supportive than on top of the water. The drawback of sculling underwater is that this same density makes it more difficult to move your paddle back and forth through your figure eights. If you have strong forearms and wrists, this will not be a problem. However, some paddlers find it too tiring and are restricted to sculling on the water's surface.

If your paddle blade begins to dive while you are sculling, don't give up or try to lift the blade out of the water suddenly. Continue to move your paddle blade and exaggerate the lift on the leading edge to bring your blade back to the surface and bring your boat back under you.

Sculling will help you build a lot of confidence in your boat balance, your paddle support, and your ability to remain upright in rough conditions. Whatever your interests are as a sea kayaker, sculling is a valuable skill in your paddling repertoire. Plus, it's great fun in its own right!

Positioning strokes

We have discussed how to go forward, how to go backward, and how to turn your boat. What if you want to go sideways, move your bow over to one side, or bring your stern back on line when surfing? You need a repertoire of strokes that position your boat in relation to other things: a dock, another boat, a wave face. To do this, you need to learn draw and ruddering strokes.

Draw strokes

With a draw stroke, you can move your boat sideways through the water. You should not lean into a draw stroke. This will slow your boat's movement, since water will pile up on that side of the boat and you'll end up bulldozing water with your boat. The best you can hope for is to maintain a flat boat as you move sideways through the water. Most paddlers are not comfortable leaning away from any stroke, so we will settle for keeping the boat flat and letting as much water pass under the boat as possible as you move sideways. Besides, most of us don't have arms long enough to lean the boat in one direction and make a draw stroke on the opposite side.

In a classic draw stroke, hold your top hand at forehead height. It becomes a fulcrum as you reach out from your hip with your lower hand to plant the blade with the powerface parallel to the boat. As you pull in toward your hip, your boat will move sideways. It may help to think of the blade being planted in the water and the boat being pulled to the blade.

Your torso should face the paddle shaft throughout the stroke as much as possible. The draw stroke requires you to have flexibility at the waist. You may feel somewhat awkward with your torso twisted around to the side of the cockpit. Be careful to keep your boat from tripping over the paddle as you pull in toward the boat.

You usually need to do more than one draw stroke at a time, so the recovery phase of this stroke is important. It is quieter and more graceful to execute the recovery phase in the water. Roll your wrist to slice the edge of the paddle away from and perpendicular to the boat to get ready for the next draw stroke. If you prefer, you may simply lift the blade out of the water to set up for the next stroke (although you won't win any "style" points!).

1. The draw stroke is made alongside your boat and parallel to your hip. Your torso should face the paddle shaft. Hold your upper hand relaxed and forehead high. **2.** The sculling draw can fine-tune the sideways motion of your boat and feels more supportive with its sculling. The boat should remain flat or be lifted slightly away from the stroke.

Hand placement on the draw stroke is important. Again, your upper hand does not travel higher than your forehead (pretend you are Scarlett O'Hara, and "swoon"). The grip on this upper hand should be loose to allow the paddle shaft to rotate back and forth. The positioning of the blade in a draw stroke is done with the lower hand. The upper hand keeps the shaft aligned and is in place in case you need a quick brace.

The best way to gain support from a draw stroke is to turn it into a sculling draw stroke. Move the paddle blade through the water alongside your boat in figure eights as you pull toward the boat. (Think of spreading that peanut butter along the side of your cockpit!) Remember to avoid leaning into this stroke, since that slows the sideward motion of your boat. Hold the lower elbow in close to your side and keep the top hand at about forehead height. The advantage of using this sculling motion is that a quick drop of the upper elbow can turn this stroke into a sculling brace when needed, the paddle shaft moving from perpendicular to parallel with the water.

You can fine-tune your sculling draw stroke so it becomes the ultimate parallel parking maneuver for slipping into tight spots. If your bow swings more than your stern, move the stroke slightly behind the cockpit. If the stern is swinging in too much, move the stroke forward of your hip. This fine adjustment is handy when the wind or boat wakes try to push you off your line.

You should power sculling draws with your torso, not your arms. Your wrists and arms will tire rapidly during a sculling draw. If you use your torso to move the paddle while keeping your arms in the same position, you will have an easier time. Sculling draws are done slowly and in a controlled manner with the paddle shaft mirroring the torso movement.

All of the draw strokes we have discussed have been made alongside your hip. We have also assumed your boat is not moving through the water but moving only as the result of your draw stroke.

What if you were paddling up to a dock and needed a last-minute adjustment to come alongside? You could accomplish this by pulling alongside the dock, stopping, and then using a draw stroke to pull into the dock. You could also use a static draw stroke, or sideslip, which takes advantage of your forward momentum and your blade angle to pull you in toward the dock without moving your paddle blade. If you plant a draw stroke alongside your boat while moving forward, the edge of the blade simply slices through the water. If you angled the leading edge of that blade out from the boat at an angle of 45 degrees or less, your boat will be pulled over and will sideslip through the water. All you are doing is holding an angled draw stroke in the catch phase as you move through the water. The water passing around the blade does the work, pulling you to your destination. You can adjust the angle of your blade depending on the direction you need to travel in. This is an eye-catching move and is fun to try.

1. To sideslip, paddle forward and plant an angled blade alongside your boat, close to your knee. **2.** Hold the planted blade at an angle so the boat is pulled toward the blade as it moves through the water.

If you take this same angled blade and move it up near your feet, you can dramatically swing your bow over. This is a handy move if you need to wind in and out of kayak traffic. You can accentuate this bow draw by leaning away from your paddle so water can easily pass under that side of the bow. The static bow draw is a wonderful boat control touch when combined with a forward stroke. It allows you to continue on your way without a break in momentum.

Don't worry about getting bogged down with the smorgasbord of draw strokes we've covered. Use a sculling draw to move your boat sideways and a regular draw stroke to look graceful and be quiet on the water. Use the other refinements, such as sideslipping and static bow draws, when you are more comfortable in your boat—when you are ready to play around with the finer points of boat control and earn some points for style!

Stern rudder strokes

As your kayak moves forward through the water, the water parts and flows down the sides of the boat. When the water reaches the widest part of the boat, it continues flowing. But an area of lower pressure is created behind this wide spot. The stern, which sits in this area of lower pressure, can now swing easily from side to side.

You can take advantage of this situation with stern rudder strokes (prys or draws), which easily set the stern over and change your boat's course. Of course, as you move the stern from side to side, the bow of your boat will move from side to side in the opposite direction.

A stern pry is set alongside the boat well behind the cockpit, and it pushes the backface of the blade out from the boat. This stroke will slow your forward momentum and move the stern away from your pry stroke. A stern pry on the right moves the bow to the right. A stern draw pulls the powerface of the blade in toward the stern and swings the stern toward the blade. A stern draw on the right moves the bow to the left.

Stern rudder strokes are very effective when you are surfing or paddling in following seas, where you must keep your boat on a line to avoid broaching (getting caught parallel to the wave). Slowing your forward momentum in this situation is not a problem. Using stern ruddering strokes while you are underway and cruising is not very helpful since you lose valuable forward momentum.

Putting it all together

As you get more comfortable in your boat, you will begin to combine strokes in a fluid manner for more effective boat handling.

You might put a quick forward sweep between your forward strokes for a snappy adjustment. You might use a bow draw to slip around an obstacle, then flawlessly move into a forward stroke to continue on your way. Paddle strokes are more than just the movements that control your boat. They become a graceful ballet on the water and are a joy to watch when done well.

• •

"I enjoy just paddling and practicing my strokes. I'll try new combinations and get the boat well up on its edge. I concentrate hard on being quiet in the water and making each move flow into the next. I do all of this in an area no bigger than a tennis court. Being able to make the boat respond to each stroke and its subtle adjustments is very satisfying."

—Linda Tatum, kayak instructor

• •

Chapter 5

ESSENTIAL SKILLS FOR
GETTING AWAY FROM IT ALL

O ne of the rewards of sea kayaking is getting away from it all. You can paddle 30 minutes from shore and be in a magical seascape—one that feels far more remote than a mere half-hour's paddle away. But getting away from it all also means leaving behind the safety nets of shoreline, harbormasters, mooring floats, and other boaters. It means taking care of yourself and others with the tools at hand: your boat, paddle, life vest, safety equipment, and—most importantly—your brain.

One of the most challenging situations you might face is an unexpected capsize by you or someone in your group. Kayak rescue techniques outline the methods for dealing with an unexpected capsize. Being able to quickly and effectively deal with these situations will make you more confident as a paddler and broaden your range of paddling choices.

Practicing these techniques just once in the safety of a pool or a calm lake is not enough. Initially, you should practice in calm conditions to get the techniques working smoothly. But once you've mastered the techniques in calm water, it is time to up the ante.

Practice solo and assisted rescue techniques on a windy day in choppy water. Choose a day with an onshore wind near a protected area that can serve as your backup site. Practice in small surf that will wash you onto a soft beach. These sea conditions will present challenges that you will never experience from textbook reading and calm-water practice. Mastering these techniques in real conditions is an invaluable exercise for you as a sea kayaker.

THE WET EXIT

Wet exit is kayaking jargon for what happens when you exit your boat following a capsize. Most sea kayakers are delighted to find that they rarely, if ever, capsize. Still, you should practice several wet exits until you are confident that you can bail out of your cockpit if needed. During wet exit practice you will probably be out of your cockpit before your head even goes underwater. Make yourself hang in there and go through all the steps of wet exit technique—you might have to fall back on these techniques when things go wrong.

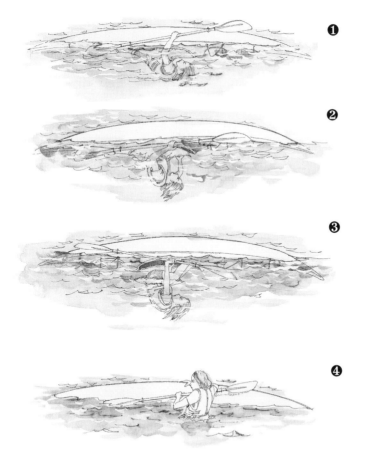

1. Lean forward and hold onto your paddle when you find yourself upside-down. 2. Pull the grab loop and clear your sprayskirt from the coaming. 3. Continue to lean forward and push your hips out of the cockpit. Your legs will follow as you forward-roll to the surface. 4. Grab your boat immediately and continue to hold your paddle.

SPRAYSKIRTS
. . . .

A sprayskirt is simply a device made of neoprene or coated nylon that fits over the cockpit opening and keeps water from getting into your boat—whether you're right side up or upside down. Imagine plopping down in your boat's cockpit while wearing one of those '50s vintage poodle skirts. The skirt would lap over the edges of the cockpit, covering the opening into the boat.

A kayak sprayskirt does the same thing, except that it's tapered to fit the cockpit opening more closely than your poodle skirt would. The sprayskirt is held around the coaming by bungee cord sewn around its edges. The front of the sprayskirt has a grab loop, usually made of webbing, that can be pulled to free the skirt from the coaming.

A sprayskirt may be a simple one designed to keep the casual wave slosh or paddle drip out of your lap, or it may be a heavy-duty version that keeps out the pounding from a surf wave. Most sprayskirts are utilitarian and are fairly boring looking. (Someone should start sewing poodles on them!). For more on sprayskirts, see Chapter 6.

The first thing to do after you've capsized is lean forward and slap your hands on your boat's hull to signal others that you've capsized. Get your face as close to your foredeck and sprayskirt grab loop as possible. This will free your hips from the seat and also protect your head if you are in shallow water or in water with underwater obstacles. Pull the grab loop of your sprayskirt forward to free it from the coaming, and then pull it back to your chest. Take the time to do a quick sweep around the coaming with your thumbs to free the sprayskirt completely. Next, place your hands beside your hips and push yourself out of the boat. Your hips and then your legs will be free from the cockpit, and your life vest flotation will bring you to the water's surface beside your boat.

As startling as an unexpected capsize is, try to remember to hold on to your paddle (one hand will do) and your boat. Retrieving equipment in wind and waves is very difficult. Never let go of your boat to retrieve other items. Swim with your boat as needed. You have just completed a wet exit.

Hanging upside down, underwater, in the dark, still in your cockpit is an unnatural situation for anyone—so it is no wonder that wet exits have this frightening aspect for many paddlers. But wet exits are simply a matter of freeing the sprayskirt from the cockpit coaming and pushing yourself out of the boat and to the surface of the water. There are only two situations that can cause a wet exit to go wrong:

- **You can't free your sprayskirt.** Before you even go paddling, practice popping your sprayskirt on land. Make sure the sprayskirt is a proper fit and that the grab loop is easy to find and pull. If it does not work properly, get another sprayskirt or fix the grab loop by adding a larger loop of webbing or a small whiffle ball you can easily grab. Always make sure the grab loop is free and clear of anything on your deck and that it is not tucked under and out of sight. Remember to do a quick thumb sweep to free the skirt from the coaming before pushing out of the cockpit.

- **You can't get your legs out of the cockpit.** You are probably leaning back and pushing out of the back of the cockpit, which locks your legs. You must lean forward and push your hips out. Then your legs will become free. If you can get in and out of your boat on land, you will certainly be able to do so with the added lubricant of water.

"**A** friend really held my hand and walked me through a wet exit and trying to roll. She is a social worker. Bart Hathaway (veteran paddler) also helped a lot—'go and see the fishes' he would say as I rolled over."

—Tamsin Venn, kayaking author and publisher of *Atlantic Coastal Kayaker*

Practicing wet exits

Your introduction to wet exits should come on your first day of instruction. You may also choose to practice them with a friend.

Your first wet exit should be dry! Get in your boat on land and practice: Pull the sprayskirt grab loop, sweep your thumbs along the coaming, and push your hips free of the cockpit. Do this again while leaning forward. Now do it with your eyes closed.

When you feel confident with your ability to free the sprayskirt, move on to calm water that's at least four feet deep so you won't hit the bottom during your exit. Make sure you are wearing your life vest. Consider wearing a pair of nose plugs to keep water out of your nose—this will help keep you from sounding like Elmer Fudd the rest of the day. If you prefer, try your first few wet exits with the sprayskirt unattached.

When you are ready to attach the sprayskirt, make sure the grab loop is clear of anything on deck. It should never be tucked under and must dangle free of the coaming. If it helps you feel more secure, have a friend stand next to your boat while you work on your exits.

After you have practiced a few wet exits, try hanging upside down in your cockpit and drumming a tune on your boat's hull before exiting. If your friend can name that tune, you get lots of style points! Now get your friend to rock the boat and splash water (it is surprisingly noisy) to simulate rougher conditions while you practice your wet exit. Play with your boat and hang upside down in the cockpit until you feel comfortable and calm every time you go over.

IT'S JUST A WATER TOY!

Instructor Tom Long helped me develop my favorite approach to the wet exit. Take the opposite tack: Try to *enter* the boat when it is partially submerged or turned over in the water. Think of the boat as something you want to stay in rather than exit.

View the boat as a water toy. Explore it from underwater. Stick your head up inside and make rude noises. Think like a kid and have fun! Once you shift your thinking, you can relax. And once you relax, you will realize you have tremendous control over your boat using your lower body and your sense of balance.

GEAR TO GET YOU BACK IN

In order to reenter your boat, or assist someone else's reentry, you will need certain pieces of safety equipment: a paddle float, a bilge pump, and a rescue sling. These should be with you every time you paddle, and they should be readily accessible—even when you are floating in the water beside your boat. Most paddlers carry this equipment under their forward deck rigging, behind their seat, or under their forward deck. After a capsize, you don't want to find this gear floating around you like a paddler's yard sale. Think carefully about your storage options.

The safety equipment needed for reentering your boat is detailed on the next page:

- **Paddle float.** A paddle float is simply a sleeve of flotation material that fits over your paddle blade. This float allows you to use your paddle as a buoyant outrigger to stabilize your boat as you reenter it from the water. There are several styles of paddle floats on the market, but the most useful is a two-chambered inflatable version. If one side blows out or malfunctions, you still have another inflatable chamber to use. A paddle float can be folded flat for easy storage, and it should have a strap or clip to prevent it from coming off the paddle blade when fully inflated.

- **Bilge pump.** A bilge pump is used to pump the water out of your boat after a capsize. A pump can be mounted in your boat, or you can carry a handheld version. If your boat has a built-in bilge pump, always make sure it is operable. Examine the pump diaphragm for cracks or holes and check the hose and exit ports for any obstructions or problems. A handheld bilge pump is by far the most economical and common version. Check it before each outing to make sure it is operating properly, and be sure it has a flotation collar.

- **Rescue sling.** After you capsize, a rescue sling can help you get a boost up onto your boat for your reentry. Rescue slings are usually about 13 feet of floating line ($\frac{5}{16}$-inch diameter or so) that has been made into a loop by joining the ends. I would recommend using a series of fisherman's knots to make your loop. (For more on knots see page 33.) The proper use of the rescue sling is covered later in this chapter, starting on page 64.

- **Life vest.** Always wear your life vest every time you go paddling. Don't just pack it—*wear it.* The buoyancy it provides is absolutely critical if you end up in the water. It is easy to put on a life vest and zip it before leaving your launch site; it's never easy to do this underway if conditions get rough. And it's nearly impossible to put one on if you're in the water, cold, and trying to hold on to a boat and a paddle. For more information on life vests, see Chapter 6, page 97.

You must stow safety gear to be easily accessible even when you are in the water alongside your boat. Here, a paddle float, bilge pump, and rescue sling are stowed under the forward deck rigging.

THE SOLO REENTRY

You must first take care of yourself. This means being able to reenter your boat after a capsize without anyone's assistance.

The first thing you should do when you bob to the surface after a capsize is grab your boat, then your paddle. On a windy day, your boat can blow away from you far faster than you can swim to retrieve it. Your boat also serves as invaluable flotation and a way to get out of cold water, even when it is overturned. Never let go of your boat during the entire process of reentry. If you move from one end of the boat to the other, you should do so with at least one hand on the boat at all times. If your boat doesn't have perimeter deck lines, you should consider adding them: Holding a deck line is far easier than holding a slippery hull.

Most paddlers find it easier to maintain a hold on a boat when it is upright. If you are not in breaking waves that could fill an exposed cockpit, give your boat a quick flip to turn it over to an upright position. A *quick* flip will result in less water being scooped into the boat. You can hook your arm through the deck lines or the rudder lines so both hands are free to manage your paddle and your paddle float. If you are concerned about waves breaking into the cockpit, keep the boat upside down. Hold the boat with your leg in the cockpit while you inflate the paddle float.

While holding onto your boat, put your paddle float on one of the paddle blades and inflate all chambers fully. Snap or clip any keeper straps on the paddle float so it stays in place. With the paddle float fully inflated and fitted over the paddle blade, place your paddle behind the rear cockpit coaming and hold it firmly with one hand

1. A quick flip of your boat will scoop less water into the cockpit. Use a strong scissors kick and push up on one side of the coaming **2.** Never lose contact with your boat. Here, the kayaker's arm is looped through a rudder line as the paddle float is inflated.

while facing the cockpit. Your paddle should be extended out at an angle perpendicular to your boat with the float on the blade farthest away from your boat.

Some boats are equipped with deck rigging just aft of the cockpit. This rigging is designed to help hold the paddle in place so you don't have to hold it with your hand. But deck rigging can fail and often is blocked by other equipment. Smaller paddlers with a short reach can also have trouble freeing the paddle from the deck rigging once they are back in the boat, and they can recapsize in the process of trying. Knowing how to reenter your boat without relying on the deck rigging will give you a backup when things don't go according to plan. Practice these reentry techniques in a variety of ways.

Your paddle with the inflated paddle float attached to its end serves as a supportive outrigger as you climb back into the boat. To get the benefit of this support, it is imperative that the paddle be extended perpendicular to the boat.

Rather than trying to chin-up onto your boat, pulling your weight vertically, flutter kick your feet to the surface behind you, moving your weight horizontally. This will help you "swim" up and onto your boat. This move is similar to swimming up to a pool edge and pulling yourself out of the water. If you get stuck part of the way up, try hooking an ankle on the paddle shaft for additional support. Don't try to ride the paddle shaft like it's a witch's broomstick—you'll overwhelm your supportive flotation and return to square one.

When you practice your paddle float reentry, try going up onto your boat both in front of and behind the paddle shaft to see which you prefer. Many paddlers like being able to reach across the cockpit to grab the coaming for help in getting up,

1. Position the paddle float perpendicular to the boat and keep it fully extended for maximum support. Flutter-kick your feet to the surface behind you and swim up and onto the boat. 2. You may choose to hook an ankle on the paddle shaft for some extra support as you swim onto the boat.

and they choose to be in front of the paddle shaft. Others prefer the lower surface of the aft deck. Just make sure you can still hold the paddle shaft with your hand throughout the process. You will need its support and will need to ensure that it stays perpendicular to the boat.

Now that you're across your boat, slowly turn so you can see your paddle float. By keeping your eyes glued to the paddle float, you will naturally favor that side with your body weight. You will also be able to make sure the float is perpendicular and fully extended from the boat. A trick for making sure you keep your weight to the supported side is to slide a hand down the paddle shaft and lean on it. Move slowly and keep your weight low—a hasty move at this point will send you back over.

You must get far enough toward the stern on your belly to get your feet into the cockpit. Once you have done this you can begin to inch backward, still on your belly, and into the cockpit until you are centered over the seat. You are now ready to turn and sit back down in your cockpit. Always turn toward the float

1. Stay low and keep your eyes on the paddle float as you work your way toward the stern. Keep both hands on the paddle and supporting most of the weight. **2.** Make the final turn to a seated position toward the side supported by your paddle float. **3.** Your weight must always favor the side supported by the paddle float. Watch the float throughout the process.

Bring the paddle shaft over your head and position it across your lap for support while pumping out the boat. Continue to favor the supported side.

and favor that side. Stay as low as possible.

Once you're seated, you will be in a cockpit that is full of water and very unstable. Before grabbing your bilge pump and getting to work, quickly bring your paddle with the float still on it over your head and place it across your lap. You can hold it in place against your belly with your elbows. This will give you support while you pump out your boat. You'll also be able to keep an eye on it at the same time. If seas are rough and you are taking on additional water as you pump, partially attach your sprayskirt before pumping. Leave just enough room for the bilge pump to be used.

After you have pumped the water out of your boat, store your safety equipment and reattach your sprayskirt. You are now ready to paddle again.

With any reentry technique, remember that you're trying to accomplish two things: getting into your boat and getting the water out of it. The order of how you do this and the actual technique you use will be determined by the conditions and by your own skill and stamina.

The paddle float reentry is a balancing act. As with any finely balanced maneuver, haste is your biggest enemy. Try to control your movements, keep your center of gravity low and close to the boat, and always remember to look at your paddle float. Remember that the conditions that caused you to capsize in the first place are probably still a factor, so your balance and control will be critical.

The solo reentry is the most difficult to accomplish and it takes the most time. But even when you are traveling with other skilled paddlers, you should know these techniques and never rely on someone else's skill to bail you out. Practicing these techniques will also give you a real confidence boost. If you are anxious about capsizing, knowing how to do these techniques will relieve those anxieties.

Using a rescue sling in your solo reentry

The rescue sling allows you to use the large, powerful muscles in your legs to get up onto the boat. This technique also helps you hold the paddle in place behind the rear coaming of the cockpit. If you have trouble getting onto the boat or holding the paddle in place during a solo reentry, consider using the rescue sling.

Rig a rescue sling to help hold the paddle in place and create a foot stirrup for an easy step up onto the boat.

You can rig the sling in conjunction with your paddle and paddle float to make a foot stirrup. Rigging the sling in this fashion also helps hold the paddle perpendicular to the boat. Once you've rigged the sling, you can step on this stirrup to boost yourself back onto your boat.

When you step onto the sling, place only the toes of your foot in the stirrup. This makes it easier to remove your foot once you're up on the boat. Once you're on top of the boat and you move toward the stern on your belly, your foot will fall out of the stirrup. Follow the same steps outlined in the solo reentry section to get back in the cockpit and seated.

You can also simply loop the sling around the coaming and let it trail in the water to become a step alongside the cockpit. This method is easy to rig, but it does not have the added advantage of holding the paddle in place behind the coaming.

Reentering a double kayak

So far, our reentry discussions have focused on single kayaks. The techniques for reentering a double kayak are not very different, but there are some subtleties that should be mentioned.

Since there are two paddlers involved, you will need to coordinate your movements. Turning the boat upright will require communication so your efforts are simultaneous. Depending on the conditions, it might be easiest for both paddlers to drape themselves across the overturned boat, grasp the cockpit edge, roll backward into the water, and pull the double kayak with them until it is upright.

Two paddlers also have an advantage as they reenter the boat: One paddler can help stabilize the boat while the other crawls back in. During the first paddler's reentry, the other paddler, still in the

GROOVING YOUR REENTRY TECHNIQUES

Too often, kayaking students practice a reentry technique once during a day of instruction and then never try it again. This is not the way to develop a skill that you will rely on, especially one you'll need in challenging conditions.

Practice your solo reentry techniques with a paddling partner. Start out in calm water and work on the movements until you can do them on automatic pilot. Play the role of instructor: Try to explain each step as you do it and point out where things could go wrong. Your paddling partner will be your attentive audience.

As you get more comfortable, practice in conditions that are a bit more challenging: wind and choppy waves. Choose a site with a soft landing and a day with an onshore breeze. Have your partner on standby in case you need help. If you can't find rougher conditions in your area, make them yourselves. Once I asked kids at the local lake to cannonball off a floating dock around the boats as students practiced reentries.

Real conditions will help you develop real responses and skills. And you are never too good to practice.

WHO GETS TO GO FIRST?

Rather than make some hard and fast rule about which paddler reenters the double kayak first, consider the following factors:

- **One paddler is decidedly weaker or less prepared for cold water immersion.** In this case, it might be wise to get that person out of the water and even enlist the help of the other paddler to do so.

- **Both paddlers are prepared for immersion but one paddler is more skilled.** Here, the more skilled paddler should consider reentering first. Once in, this person can do a sculling brace to stabilize the boat for the second paddler's reentry.

- **Both paddlers are equally skilled and prepared for immersion.** In this scenario, consider allowing the stern paddler to reenter first. From the stern position, she can see and better assist the second paddler's reentry.

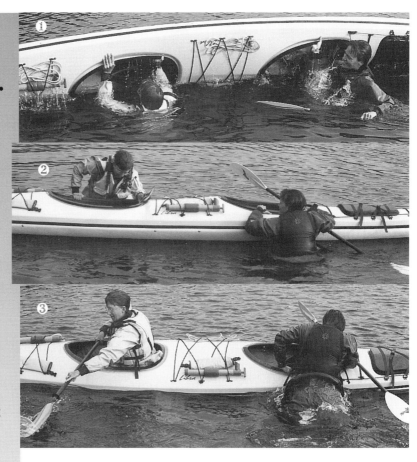

1. Flipping a double kayak upright requires the coordinated effort of two paddlers. **2.** One paddler should stabilize the boat while the other paddler crawls aboard. **3.** The second paddler enters while the first uses a sculling brace (here, a low one) for support.

water, can counterbalance the weight from the other side of the boat. The other paddler can also drape herself across the deck of the boat. When the second paddler reenters the boat, the first paddler sitting in her cockpit can do a sculling brace to help stabilize the boat.

You can use a paddle float on a double kayak reentry if you need it to stabilize the boat. There also is a decided advantage to carrying two bilge pumps. A rescue sling is another tool that can be used if needed.

THE ASSISTED REENTRY

Being able to enlist the aid of another paddler after a capsize is a definite advantage. This person is out of the water and has additional pieces of safety equipment. She can also counterbalance your reentry and help corral any wayward pieces of gear.

Just like in the solo reentry, you are trying to accomplish two things in an assisted reentry: getting someone back into the boat and getting the water out of it. How you do this and in what order will be determined by the actual conditions. Surf or extremely cold conditions may necessitate immediate reentry. If conditions are less extreme, you may delay reentry and empty the boat first.

There are many assisted reentry techniques, each with its own advantages and disadvantages. If you practice several different techniques, you will have a formidable repertoire to fall back on when things go wrong. Remember that the rescuer's size does not matter in these techniques. At no point do you need to lift anyone from the water. Instead, you are counterbalancing the other person's weight with your own boat and body position as she climbs back aboard. Throughout our discussion of the rescue process, I will refer to the capsized paddler as the swimmer.

Remember the following for good assisted reentry technique:

- **Speak to the swimmer in a calm, confident voice.** Take charge of the situation and keep instructions simple.

- **Make sure the swimmer holds onto the boat at all times.** If the swimmer becomes separated from her boat, the situation becomes more difficult. Now you have to retrieve both a boat and a swimmer. Make sure the swimmer also holds onto her paddle until you are ready to take it.

- **Before approaching closely, determine if the swimmer is uninjured and coherent.** You don't need to be capsized by a panic-stricken swimmer. You also need to determine if there is an injury or some other factor that may determine your choice of rescue technique. Talk to the swimmer and get answers to simple questions: Are you okay? Are you getting cold? Do you have your paddle?

- **A swimmer who is cold and not prepared for cold water immersion must be dealt with immediately.** Get the swimmer out of the water by having her lie across the stern of the overturned boat or across your stern deck. Communicate constantly to monitor her condition. Minimize her time in the cold water.

- **Get to the capsized boat at any angle you can and grab it.** Don't waste time trying to paddle into a perfect position. It is much easier and faster to grab the capsized boat, lean into it, and—using your hands—maneuver your own boat around the capsized boat.

- **Consider the tools you have at hand.** The tools you have access to are your boat, paddle, paddle float, rescue sling, bilge pump, and possibly another paddler in the group. You might elect to use some or all of these invaluable tools depending on the conditions.

- **Remember that the swimmer's boat offers stable flotation.** You can lean on or across the swimmer's boat and be completely stable as you help her reenter the boat.

- **Once the swimmer is back in the boat, make sure she is ready to resume paddling before you let go of her boat.** Unless you have to get out of a given area quickly, hold onto her until you are absolutely sure she is ready to go. Make certain her gear is accounted for and operable. Check to see if she needs any additional clothing, fluids, or a snack.

As I cover the following techniques, I will assume that the steps above have been followed unless otherwise noted.

T-rescue variations

The **T**-shakeout rescue is the assisted rescue technique I have used repeatedly as a guide and instructor. It can be completed in less than one minute (an advantage in cold Maine waters), and it allows you to keep an eye on the rescued person throughout the process. With this technique you can empty the boat of water before the swimmer reenters it.

Before lifting the overturned boat, position the two boats in a **T** formation. This configuration is the most stable for the rescuer.

To begin a **T**-shakeout rescue, grab the overturned boat anywhere you can and position yourself at its bow. Have the swimmer go to the stern. If there is no rudder or skeg (which provide easy clues about which end of the overturned boat is which), you can tell which end is which by looking for the footbrace screws; they are closer to the bow.

Once you are at the bow, you no longer need your paddle. Store it under your deck rigging where it will be out of the way but easy to retrieve. Swing your own boat perpendicular to the overturned boat to form a **T**. If possible, have the swimmer push down on the stern of the overturned boat as you lift the bow onto your cockpit. Lifting the boat is still possible without the swimmer's help, but the push down at the stern helps break the vacuum as the cockpit clears the water. With the bow of the overturned boat positioned in your lap, lift the bow until the cockpit is above the water. This will enable you to spill the water out of the boat.

When the boat is empty, roll the bow in your hands until the boat is upright in the water. Make sure you don't scoop any water into the cockpit during this step. Pull your boat alongside the emptied boat and face your boat in the opposite direction (that is, your bow will be at the emptied boat's stern).

The swimmer can now come alongside her boat and prepare to climb back in. Take the swimmer's paddle and store it alongside your own. To stabilize her boat, lean across it and grab the thighbraces or two edges of the cockpit coaming with both hands. Coach the swimmer through the reentry: Have her stay low and on her belly as she works toward the stern and gets her feet into the cockpit. Then she can back into the cockpit and, turning toward you, sit down.

The **T**-shakeout rescue can only be used on boats with a rear bulkhead. On a boat with a rear bulkhead, the bow lift sends the water rushing toward the stern. The water hits the rear bulkhead, which is just behind the seat, and spills out of the boat.

If the capsized boat does not have bulkheads, drag the overturned boat across the cockpit of your boat until its center point is in front of you. This is called a **TX** rescue. In the **TX** version, you allow the water to run out from both ends of the boat as you balance the boat on your cockpit and rock it back and forth with a seesaw motion.

The swimmer may help by pushing down on the stern while the bow is lifted and the water drained from the cockpit.

Once the rescued boat is upright, the rescuer leans towards the swimmer's boat and swings her own boat parallel to it.

T-rescue tips

The following tips can be used in **T**-rescue procedures:

- **Position the boats in opposite directions.** This positioning has several advantages. You have convenient handholds on the front of the cockpit. You can also keep an eye on the person throughout the rescue. Working from the cockpit's front end,

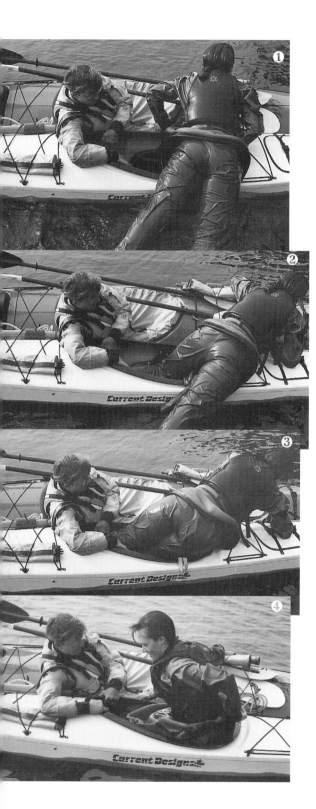

1. The rescuer uses both hands to stabilize the swimmer's boat as she climbs aboard. This is a very stable position even if the swimmer were much larger than the rescuer. **2.** The rescuer stabilizes the swimmer's boat with both hands and her torso while coaching the swimmer back into the cockpit of the boat. **3.** As she turns to sit down in the cockpit, the swimmer turns toward the rescuer's boat. **4.** While the rescued swimmer attaches her sprayskirt and readies herself to resume paddling, the rescuer should continue to stabilize the boat.

you'll have less chance of your getting your fingers smashed behind a seatback or under the person.

- **Check the rudder cables of the overturned boat.** While the swimmer is at the stern, have her check the rudder cables on her boat to make sure everything is in its proper place. It is common to get rudder cables crossed or have other troublesome snags occur during a capsize. It is easiest to fix them at this point, assuming the swimmer is capable of helping and not in danger from cold water.

- **Secure your own paddle during the rescue.** Once you grab the overturned boat, you won't need your paddle until the rescue is complete. Tuck it securely underneath your deck rigging on the side away from the overturned boat. If you use a paddle leash, simply drop your paddle in the water on the outside of your boat (see more on paddle leashes in Chapter 6, page 93).

- **Use the overturned boat as your outrigger for support.** When you begin to lift the overturned boat's bow out of the water, you may feel unsteady. Commit both hands to the bow and hold on tight. Even if you lose your balance, that overturned boat is like a 17-foot outrigger for support. Hold onto it and you will not have a problem.

- **Secure the swimmer's paddle.** You may take the swimmer's paddle at any point and stow it under your deck rigging. It is advantageous to take the swimmer's paddle before she climbs back onto the boat. Otherwise, there is a good chance you'll get hit with it.

- **Always hang onto the swimmer's boat.** Simply leaning across the swimmer's boat is not sufficient, especially in rough conditions. Unless you need to help pull the swimmer aboard, you should use both hands to grasp inside of the cockpit coaming (preferably on the thighbraces) for the best handholds. Don't hesitate to drape your torso across the foredeck of the swimmer's boat as you hold onto the cockpit.

- **Use a sling if necessary.** If the swimmer needs assistance getting back on the boat, you can rig a sling around the coaming of her boat for an easy step up.

If you need to, you can resort to a simple reenter and pump rescue that foregoes the emptying part of T-style rescue. Simply pull alongside the overturned boat, turn it over, and get the person back in. The swimmer's boat will be unstable until you can get the water out. But if you are in surf or about to be pushed into an obstacle like a ledge or a jetty, it may be best to get the person back in and try to exit the area. Once you are a safe distance

1. The swimmer may enter her boat from a position *between* the two boats. She drapes her arms over each boat for support. **2.** The swimmer leans back and swings her legs up into the cockpit while the rescuer stabilizes the boat with both hands. **3.** The swimmer slides into the cockpit and seats herself. The rescuer continues to stabilize the boat until the swimmer is ready to resume paddling.

WHAT NOW?

. . . .

For the filming of our kayak rescue video *What Now?*, my husband Vaughan and I decided to demonstrate all the assisted rescues with me as the rescuer and Vaughan as the swimmer. Vaughan is 6'4" and weighs 220 pounds. I am 5'4" and weigh 125 pounds. When teaching rescues, we both found that students were concerned about the size differences between a rescuer and a swimmer. Couples often entered the class unconvinced that the wife could rescue the husband. (Of course, they often erroneously assumed that the wife would be the one who needed to be rescued in the first place.)

By showing that size disparity was not an issue in a rescue, we convinced students that they could rescue someone nearly twice their size. This gave them a real confidence boost.

away, you can then raft back up to pump the water from the boat.

In another variation of a **T**-rescue technique, you can bring a swimmer aboard from a position between the two boats. Have the swimmer come between the two boats with one arm over each boat's stern deck. When she is near the cockpit, have the swimmer lean back, swing her legs up and into the cockpit, and then scoot in. The rescuer holds the boat the same way as described before. Some people find this method works well, and others are unable to do it at all. Either way, you now have one more option when dealing with a capsize situation.

Learning these variations of assisted rescue techniques will give you a solid foundation for dealing with a capsize when paddling with others. You now know three different ways to empty water out of an overturned boat: **T**-shakeout, **TX,** and reenter and pump (no **T**). You also now know different ways of helping a person back aboard: using their own power or rigging a rescue sling. You also have a paddle float on standby if you need to further stabilize the boat for any reason.

The scoop rescue

If you are a disabled paddler or you paddle with someone who is disabled, you should learn a scoop rescue. This rescue is also useful when someone is seriously injured or unconscious. However, my description for the scoop rescue relates only to a disabled paddler. The other scenarios are medical ones that entail emergency protocol not within the scope of this book. See the Resources section, page 153, for recommended reading on wilderness medicine procedures.

When you do a scoop rescue, you position your boat alongside the swimmer's boat. You need to get the swimmer's boat on its side and partially submerged. When the boat is on its side, you are on the non-cockpit side. In this on-edge position, the swimmer can get herself inside from the water, feet first. When you do this, you must hold onto the swimmer's boat and lean across it. You may have to help tuck the swimmer into the cockpit.

Once the swimmer is in the cockpit, pull the boat back upright. This will require you to reach across the cockpit and

The scoop rescue partially submerges the swimmer's cockpit and scoops her into it. Then the rescuer leans back to pull the swimmer and her boat upright.

roll back with the swimmer's boat until it is upright. In essence, the swimmer is "scooped" up out of the water while she is in her cockpit. The swimmer can help you by shifting her weight in your direction or even by pulling her weight up with her hands on your boat. It helps to have another paddler positioned on your other side to stabilize your boat and act as a counterweight in the process.

Assisted reentry techniques for double kayaks

The same principles and many of the same procedures used for single kayaks can be used for double kayaks. The main differences are that you now have two paddlers to get back into the boat, and you will not be able to lift a double and empty it prior to the swimmers reentering it.

Have bilge pumps and bailers ready for use and continue to stabilize the double kayak while the water is being emptied out. Double kayaks can take on a great deal of water in a capsize, so you will have your work cut out for you. But the pumping can conceivably be shared by at least three paddlers. Like the other assisted rescue techniques, you can use rescue slings, paddle floats, and other gear—depending on the conditions.

GOOD COMMUNICATION

If someone in your paddling group capsizes, it is time to act. You should immediately paddle to the area of the capsize. If there is a more experienced paddler in the group, follow her lead and give her the assistance she requests. You can be useful rounding up wayward gear or keeping an eye on the rest of the group. Stay out of the way of the actual reentry process.

If you are in the role of rescuer, take charge. Stay calm and use very confident, short statements or questions when you speak to the swimmer. She may try to take charge of the situation; if she does, ask her clearly to listen to you. State what you are doing at each step.

A sudden capsize is often very embarrassing to the swimmer. Reassure her that it's no big deal. She may even be laughing at herself. Laugh with her and tell her she'll get her turn with you next.

Some paddlers, finding themselves unexpectedly in the water, are completely unnerved. They may choke up and may not follow directions. You need to stay cool and help calm them. (Even if *your* heart is pounding, act like you've done this a hundred times.) In this situation the swimmer is more likely to let go of her boat, so repeat over and over, "Don't let go of your boat; please hang on to your boat." Make this your mantra until you get her back in the boat.

THE ESKIMO ROLL

The easiest way to deal with a capsize is to remain in your boat and roll it back up underneath you. This is called the Eskimo roll. The roll is very fast, your exposure to cold water is minimized, and you are not in danger of becoming separated from your boat or other equipment.

Rolling a kayak is not a new technique. This skill was developed by early paddlers in harsh environments. For these kayakers, exiting the boat into icy water wasn't a viable option.

Learning to roll your boat is definitely a skill you should pursue. It is useful, even graceful, and fun to do. Mastering the Eskimo roll is one of the biggest confidence boosters you can give yourself as a kayaker. However, no roll is 100 percent assured. You still need to be proficient with solo and assisted rescues.

There are many rolling methods and styles. Some aficionados claim to be able to execute at least 20 different varieties—and therein lies the fun of rolling! You can switch sides, hold your paddle differently, and do all sorts of underwater maneuvering and fancy tricks. Rolling is play-time.

In this book, I will not attempt to cover all rolling techniques. But I will give you the basics and some tips so you can get started. The best way to learn how to roll is through an instructional program. When you're learning to roll it is easy to become disoriented and be unable to give your-self accurate feedback on your movements. Having an instructor alongside is invaluable. She can observe your position and movements and give you the feedback you need. A video critique of your rolling practice is also a big help. Find an instruction program that has this capacity or ask if you can bring your own video camera and have someone tape you.

The roll can be broken down into two stages. The first phase is the set-up, which requires you to bring your body and paddle into position for the actual roll. The second phase is the combination of body and paddle movements that brings your boat underneath you as you come to the surface.

In most common rolls, the set-up phase requires that you get your paddle above the surface of the water while your boat is overturned. It is easiest to do this by bringing your paddle parallel to and close to the boat. Think of punching your paddle up to the sky with your arms, which will get the paddle above the surface of the water. You are now set up for a roll.

Think back to how you practiced braces. You slapped and sculled your paddle for support as you leaned the boat over and then brought it back underneath you. The roll is really the same idea: You are just starting from a completely overturned position.

You will either need to slap the surface of the water perpendicular to the boat in a high brace position (C-to-C roll) or sweep the surface from bow to stern in a forward sweep position (sweep roll) as you swing your hips to bring the boat underneath you. Remember your head dink. It will free your hips to roll the boat up. Dropping your head makes it easier to get your torso up with the boat. It helps to look at the working paddle blade throughout the roll. Your head should be the last thing to leave the water, even though it wants to be the first!

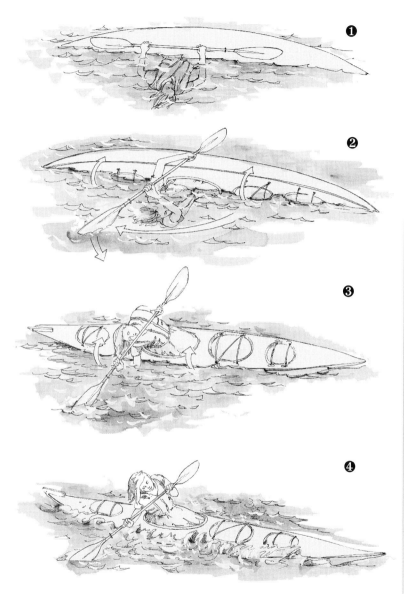

1. Set up for your C-to-C roll by punching the paddle skyward alongside your boat. You should feel air on your wrists. **2.** Position the paddle in a high brace position with the working blade above or as close to the surface as possible. **3.** Snap your hip and lift your knee to bring the boat back underneath you as you gain support from the downward slap of your paddle blade. **4.** Your head is the last thing to leave the water and should only be lifted when you are fully upright. You will finish in a high brace position facing forward.

ROLLING AND CONFIDENCE
• • • • • • • • • • • • • • • • • • •

I'll let you in on a little secret—very few sea kayakers really know how to roll. Oh sure, among instructors it's standard fare. But most sea kayakers don't—or won't—learn how to roll their boats. They'll almost certainly be fine, but they'll always be limited.

Rolling is one of the best ways to build confidence in your abilities as a kayaker. If you don't learn to roll, you'll never experience this heady feeling. You're looser and more relaxed on the water, and you see many paddling challenges as potential playtime rather than hazards to avoid. For years I could roll with ease. I never doubted my roll skills, so I was happy to turn my boat over for any reason—I knew I could roll it back up.

Then I lost my roll! To this day I don't know where it went, but it took a lot of my confidence with it. I felt like Steve Sax, the Los Angeles Dodgers' second baseman who, for an entire season, lost his ability to make a simple throw to first base. Rolling became for me, like Sax's throw, a traumatic mind game. The more I tried, the worse I got.

continued on page 76

continued from page 75

For a while I thought, forget it, I don't need this skill. After all, outside of kayak surfing, I never capsized by mistake. But I missed rolling! And more importantly, I missed the confidence and bravado it gave me. I swallowed my pride and asked for instruction. I'm back rolling, and I think it was a great decision!

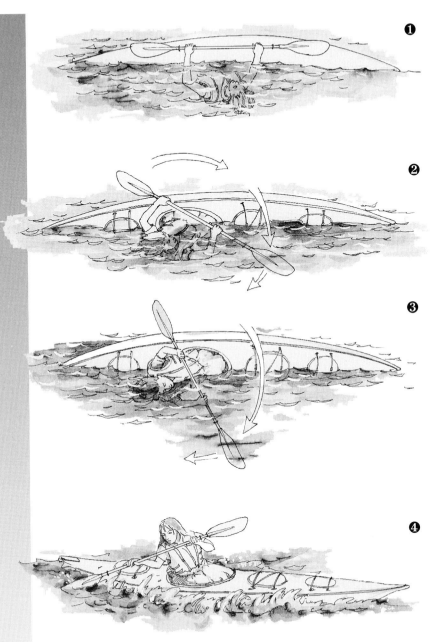

1. To set up for the sweep roll, punch the paddle skyward and alongside your boat. 2. Begin your blade's sweeping motion with a climbing angle on the leading edge of the blade for lift and support. 3. As you move through your sweep, snap your hips to bring the boat underneath you. 4. As you complete the sweep roll make sure the paddle blade is out of the water at the stern. At the finish of the sweep roll, you will be leaning slightly back and turned toward the working side.

Once you have learned how to roll, practice it every time you go paddling. If you're a ham, pop off a few rolls at your launch site—you're sure to draw a crowd. If the water is cold and you want to stay dry, save the rolls for the end of the day. But practice, practice, practice!

Illustrations on pages 75 and 76 show the positions and paddle movements for both the C-to-C roll and the sweep roll—two of the most common rolls for kayakers.

Teaching aids

One method for learning a roll is to place a paddle float on one blade for additional support until you learn the positions and movements of the roll. If you use a dual-chamber paddle float, inflate only the chamber on the backface of the blade. This way, you can still get a good climbing angle if you are practicing a sweep roll. As you get more comfortable, let more and more air out of the paddle float until you are no longer dependent on it.

Another way to gain additional support while learning a roll is to extend your paddle. Instead of using your usual centered, shoulder-width grip, hold the paddle by one blade and use the fully extended paddle for support during your roll. This may feel clumsy, but you'll be surprised at the additional support it will give you.

When learning how to roll, use a dive mask or nose plugs. You'll avoid getting water up your nose and will be able to look around to get oriented. You can monitor your paddle blade position with a mask. And you can make sure your head is the last thing to leave the water by continuing to look at the paddle blade until you feel the boat completely under you. Now, you're ready to roll!

YOUR EQUIPMENT

So far I have focused on the techniques you need for paddling and enjoying the sport. I've discussed equipment only in its generic form. But now it's time to get down to specifics and focus on the actual gear you hold, lift, wear, and sit in and on.

In this chapter you will learn about selecting the right kayak, paddle, and safety equipment for your needs—as well as how to care for the gear you choose. When selecting gear, I highly recommend you buy the best equipment you can afford for your intended use. Good gear is worth every penny you pay for it. If your needs change, sell your equipment and get what you want. The resale value of sea kayaking equipment is excellent. Don't worry that you'll get stuck with a garage full of equipment you've outgrown. You might also want to hold onto your old gear as spares for friends and family.

Too often women end up purchasing gear that is unsuitable for them. The equipment models chosen for instructional and touring programs are often the ones that fit the widest range of people and are the most available. People on either end of the size range suffer: Larger paddlers are faced with the discomfort of a tight fit, and smaller paddlers are put in boats that swallow them and make the going tougher than it needs to be. It is important to have equipment that fits you and allows you to realize your potential as a paddler—not prevent it!

The good news is that manufacturers are listening to feedback from women who have been frustrated in their search for good equipment. Keep the pressure on.

KAYAKS

The first step in choosing a kayak that is suitable for you is to remember the questions you asked yourself in Chapter 2 (page 17). First and foremost, your kayak must do what you need it to do. No single boat model will do everything well: One that travels efficiently on open water will not turn on a dime in a winding backwater marsh; one you can use as a stable platform for fishing and photography will not feel snappy or be quick to accelerate in surf.

As sea kayaking becomes more popular, more and more boat models appear in the marketplace. Choosing a boat has become a complex, sometimes difficult decision. You'll be tempted to want a boat that does everything well, but you'll have to determine priorities. Identify your primary use for a kayak and choose one that's designed for that purpose. You can always consider a second boat later for other activities.

In this book we're focusing on sea kayaks and, to some extent, recreational kayaks, the sea kayak's simpler cousin. Recreational kayaks are at home on lakes and ponds, but you must be cautious about venturing farther afield in them. With their simple designs, they often lack the fortitude to go to sea.

The stuff they're made of

Before looking at different models of sea kayaks, you should know something about what they are made of. The materials used to make kayaks determine a boat's cost, weight, and performance.

"**M**y first sea kayak set-up, as I look back after a three-year, sometimes frustrating search for properly fitting equipment, was ludicrously disproportionate to my body size. I'm of the small-but-tall variety, weighing in at about 107 pounds after a fully clothed wet exit, and topping out at 5'7"; I have an average trunk height, long thighs but narrow hips and shoulders. So there I sat in my 17-foot, 24½-inch beam boat, wallowing in a PFD that rode up to my chin and chafed my armpits, enshrouded by a huge sprayskirt that puckered and sagged in the middle and let a steady drip-drip-drip into my lap from the pooled water, and flailing away with a 240-cm. large-bladed paddle. No wonder I was always bringing up the rear of the group, but, hey, I figured it was because I'm simply smaller and weaker, right? . . ."

—paddler Roseann Hanson, from *The Whole Paddler's Catalog*, edited by Zip Kellogg

● ●

"I like a boat that is sleek, fast, and light and that tracks well. Being able to lift my boat myself is also very important. I like a padded cockpit; as a small person, this helps immensely with boat control. Also, a comfortable seat with good lumbar support is essential."

—Pam Sweeney, manager, Winnipesaukee Kayak Co.

● ●

Kayaks are generally made of one of two types of material: polyethylene (a type of plastic) or layers of resin and cloth (usually fiberglass or Kevlar).

Polyethylene boats

Polyethylene boats are mass-produced from enormous rotomolding machinery, which rotates and seesaws a boat mold so molten plastic flows and coats the interior. The mold is removed from the oven, and the boat is popped out, cooled, and outfitted.

Polyethylene is very durable. Direct hits to the hull or constant grinding on rocky beaches don't phase it. Kids can jump on it, adults can drag it along a beach, and your dog can scramble up the side without causing any noticeable damage. Polyethylene is also the most affordable material for making kayaks.

The drawbacks of polyethylene are weight, inherent flexibility, and aesthetics. The heavier weight of polyethylene requires more effort on the water than a lighter, composite boat. Weight is also a significant factor when you move the boat around on land. Polyethylene boats will flex to some extent, and this flex wastes some of your effort as you paddle. It is also more difficult to mold sharp lines in polyethylene. A sharp stem that parts the water cleanly may become thickened and blunter when made of polyethylene, affecting both efficiency and aesthetics. Over the last decade, however, polyethylene boats have become more rigid and of finer design. Buyers have demanded higher quality, and the materials and manufacturing processes have also advanced.

Composite boats

Boats made from cloth and resin are called composite boats. Composite sea kayaks are usually made of either fiberglass cloth and resin or Kevlar cloth and resin. The primary differences between fiberglass and Kevlar versions are weight and cost.

Composite boats are made by layering cloth and resin to create a composite material that is rigid and has a high strength-to-weight ratio. This layering of cloth and resin can be done by hand or under vacuum pressure (to minimize the amount of resin used). Each manufacturer has its own secret blend of resin and pattern for cloth placement and reinforcement. What is important for you is the lighter weight and rigidity composite boats offer.

A polyethylene boat will weigh 7 to 12 pounds more than its counterpart made of fiberglass and resin. A total of 7 pounds may not sound like a lot of weight, but 7 pounds removed from a 60-pound boat is significant. The weight savings may bring a boat within your range for solo lifting.

The same boat model in two different materials. The composite boat **(left)** shows sleeker lines and a finer entry than its polyethylene sister **(right).**

Composite boats also have a sleek beauty that is impossible to replicate in polyethylene. The method of manufacturing composite boats allows for finer hull designs with sharper entry and exit points. These finer lines are not only an aesthetic consideration, they also affect performance. A sharp entry minimizes turbulence as the boat parts the water. The smooth construction and rigidity of composite boats help the boat move through the water efficiently.

Within composite methods, you may choose fiberglass or Kevlar cloth. Kevlar cloth is lighter and somewhat more puncture resistant than fiberglass cloth. It is also more expensive. A comparable Kevlar-cloth model will sell for $350 to $500 more than its fiberglass-cloth counterpart. The use of Kevlar cloth can also reduce the weight of a single kayak by another 5 to 10 pounds.

The downside of composite boats is their additional expense. They average about $1,000 more than their polyethylene counterparts. Composite boats, especially dark-colored ones, show scratches more easily than plastic boats do. And composite boats may crack or fracture if you severely mistreat them. I have never babied my composite boats, and they are scratched and chipped from years of playing in the surf and other abuses. Still, they are a long way from fragile.

The color on composite boats comes from an outer layer of gelcoat, a pigmented resin. Gelcoat also adds a layer of protection and UV resistance. Because the hull and the deck are made separately in composite boats, you have a wide choice when it comes to colors for the two halves.

As you navigate the apparent maze of kayak materials, benefits, and prices, refer to the table on page 82. It's a useful guide to general price ranges for kayaks of various sizes, weights, and structures.

Additional options

In addition to polyethylene and composite boats, there are other types of sea kayaks: inflatable models and those that can be disassembled for storage (folding kayaks). These styles offer the convenience of easy land storage (a closet or car trunk can work fine). They can also travel with you to some far-flung destination.

Sea kayaks at a glance						
Type	**Material**	**Price range**	**Length (ft.)**	**Weight (lbs.)**	**Benefits**	**Drawbacks**
single	polyethylene	$800–$1,500	14–19	48–68	durable; least expensive	heavier; least efficient
single	fiberglass	$1,700–$2,600	14–19	42–57	lighter; sleeker; efficient	more expensive; shows scratches and scrapes; may need repairs more often than polyethylene version
single	Kevlar	$2,400–$3,100	14–19	37–50	even lighter; more puncture resistant	expensive; repairs may be trickier to blend than fiberglass repairs;
double	polyethylene	$1,500–$2,000	16–18	78–110	same as single	same as single; length limited by manufacturing process
double	fiberglass	$2,600–$3,300	18–22	79–95	same as single	same as single
double	Kevlar	$3,000–$4,200	18–22	70–84	same as single	same as single

Inflatable kayaks are a great choice if storage is limited or if you need portability when traveling to your launching points. (Courtesy of Innova Group)

Folding kayaks have a framework of aluminum or wood. You can reconstruct this frame at your paddling site and stretch the material skin on the frame to form the kayak. They include inflatable sponsons along the sides, which when fully inflated add flotation and rigidity to the boat.

You can also choose an inflatable kayak. This type of boat is easier to ready at the water's edge, but it may not offer the rigidity of the best folding varieties. Inflatables have come a long

You may choose to build your own kayak. Here, a fabric skin is being stitched over its wooden frame by Donna Ingersoll, a student at Superior Kayak's School of Traditional Kayaks. (Courtesy of Scott Ingersoll)

way from the vinyl dime-store rafts of the past. Today, inflatables are made of tough, abrasion-resistant materials. Some touring models even sport rudders.

Skin-on-frame models are also available in many traditional designs. Even though modern versions of this type of boat may use a treated canvas skin and a tubular aluminum frame instead of steam-bent wooden ribs and seal skins, these boats still say a lot about the history of sea kayaking. These designs are timeless in their elegance and seaworthiness—regardless of the materials used to make them. Many homemade kits and plans are available for building your own skin-on-frame boat. You can also attend a workshop where you build your own traditional kayak under the guidance of a master builder.

The art and science of sea kayak design

In Chapter 3, I discussed kayaks in their generic form. But a sea kayak is a personal matter. Your style as a kayaker is defined by the interaction between the inanimate (boat) and the animate (paddler).

A sea kayak is your backpack on the water. You pack it with gear and move it from place to place as you explore to your heart's content. You will be surprised by the amount of gear you can pack in your boat. Traveling by sea kayak is far more luxurious than backpacking, since the weight of your gear is less of an issue when it is supported by water.

Designed to withstand rough-water crossings and maintain a course in challenging seas and wind, single sea kayaks generally range from 14 to 19 feet long. If the boat was any shorter, you would find it difficult to maintain a course over much distance. Your storage capacity would also be minimal.

Your personal tastes and how the boat fits you will be major factors in your boat choice. There are other factors to also consider when making your choice:

- **Bulkheads and flotation.** Most sea kayaks have forward and aft bulkheads that confine to the cockpit any water you take on during a capsize. This makes the boat easier to empty. The storage compartments formed by these bulkheads keep your gear dry and in place. Some earlier models and smaller models use flotation bags in place of bulkheads reducing your storage capacity and the overall cost of the boat. Inflatable bags called flotation bags are used to fill these open ends of the boat. With flotation bags, the areas they fill cannot take on large amounts of water. These bags must be inflated and held in place so they will not float free if you capsize or enter rough seas. If you purchase a sea kayak without bulkheads, you must have flotation bags in your boat. A store or manufacturer will occasionally sell boats without these bags. They assume you will find and purchase a flotation bag on your own. This is a dangerous practice that has caused several accidents when new boat owners—either due to ignorance or in the interest of saving money—did not purchase flotation bags for their boats.

- **Tracking ability.** If you are going to paddle on open water (*i.e.*, on large lakes or on the ocean), your boat's ability to hold its course in wind and waves is critical. However, a boat that tracks well will not be quick to turn without changing its hull configuration. You can do this by leaning the boat on edge. Conversely, a boat that feels maneuverable will not hold its course as well as the boat that tracks straight as an arrow. When choosing a boat, remember this: A solid tracking boat can be made maneuverable with your skills as a paddler, but a maneuverable boat can only be made into a better tracking boat by using a rudder or with a lot of work on your part. A rudder adds complexity and some drawbacks in performance (dragging anything off the stern is something of a burden). The boat length you choose will also be affected by these factors, since longer boats enhance tracking and efficiency.

- **Rudders versus skegs.** Instead of a rudder, some boats have a retractable skeg. This skeg drops down from the aft part of the hull and is controlled by a slider next to the cockpit. A real advantage to a skeg is that you can control how deeply you drop its blade; a rudder, on the other hand, is an all-or-nothing proposition. Also, a skeg allows your footbraces to remain in a locked position for full support. When a rudder is dropped, the footbraces slide with each push of your foot, and you need to learn to balance the pressure on each side to have their full support. The downside of a skeg is that the skeg box—the area that holds the retractable skeg blade—takes up a significant amount of space in the boat's rear storage compartment. Skegs, like rudders, can sometimes break or jam. Take care to keep small pebbles and sand from blocking the skeg's movement.

- **On-deck features.** The deck of your sea kayak should have various pieces of bungee cord running across it (deck rigging). You can use this deck rigging to hold

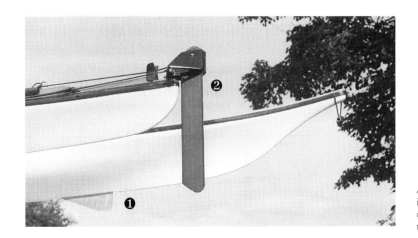

A skeg **(1)** is dropped from the hull and is fixed in position. A rudder blade **(2)** is dropped from the stern and can be moved side to side.

charts and other essentials in front of you on the foredeck. Placed on the aft deck, these lines will allow you to carry a spare paddle, some camping equipment, or even your favorite fishing rod.

If the boat does not have perimeter deck lines, you should add them. These lines, running the length of the boat on each side, make it easy for you to grab your boat in the event of a capsize. If your boat has rudder lines along the aft deck, you may prefer to add perimeter lines only to the foredeck.

You can carry a compass on the foredeck. The compass should be in a spot that allows you to read it easily at a glance and then look straight ahead. Some kayaks have compasses permanently mounted in the deck. You can also use a removable version that clips across the deck. The compass should be mounted on the centerline of your boat. When you pack your boat, make sure that anything metal—your VHF radio, flashlight, or skillet—is kept well away from the compass. If the metal objects are too close to your compass, they can cause deviation in your compass readings.

How the boat reacts to you

How a boat feels is primarily determined by how the boat fits you and how it reacts to your presence.

You must be comfortable in your cockpit for hours at a stretch. Your hips, thighs, and knees will maintain contact with the boat during this time. You should have ample foot room and be able to shift and relax your position when needed. Run your hand around the inside of the boat to make sure the finished surface is smooth and free from any plastic or cloth splinters. At some point, you will probably want to customize the fit of your boat (see "Customizing your boat," pages 88–89).

How the boat reacts to you on the water is determined by the interplay of your build and weight distribution, the boat's hull design, and the paddling conditions.

When I first started trying out kayaks, I was drawn to a particular style of boat. (I won't tell you which one!) The boat I was drawn to looked quick and nimble, and I could easily imagine myself in it. I had seen several good paddlers in this type of boat, and I was convinced that it was the boat for me. But every time I tried one, I was uncomfortable and nothing hit me in the right places. I kept insisting on trying, assuring myself that I had gotten an odd one out of the batch. After a couple of months of torturing myself, I finally gave up and tried other boats for their comfort and paddling characteristics. I can say that I'm happy with my decision. The lesson I learned is that the perfect boat for your friend is not necessarily the perfect boat for you.

"To weed out boats that are a poor fit, sit relaxed in a kayak. If your elbows are touching the coaming, that kayak is too big or deep for you. You should eliminate it and continue to try only the ones that pass the elbow test."

—Judy Moyer

For example, a single kayak's beam (its maximum width) may range from 20.5 to 25 inches. Narrower boats generally feel less stable than wider boats. But the actual hull configuration dictates how a given width feels to you. Once you know a boat's beam, look at the boat's footprint on the water. Think of getting into a boat and capturing the boat's footprint in wet cement. How much area does the boat take up on the water with you in it?

Two 17-foot boats with identical beams may have very different footprints on the water and, as a result, feel very different. One boat may narrow quickly from its beam to sharp exit and entry lines, and the second boat may narrow gradually from its beam. The first boat will feel sportier and quicker to accelerate; the latter will have a greater area amidships and will feel stable and slower to reach cruising speed.

Sea kayak hull shapes are varied, and the shape will tell you a lot about how a boat will feel initially. If you view the cross section of a boat at its widest part, the hull may range from rounded vee to very shallow vee. This shape will often overshadow the hard numbers of width. For example, a rounded hull with a 23-inch beam may feel much less reassuring than a hull that is 21 inches wide and has some flare built into its shallow vee bottom. The added flare creates more surface area on the water without increasing the beam. This makes the boat feel more stable.

Your body shape and size will accentuate or lessen certain hull characteristics of a kayak. A long, wide torso with a high center of gravity may accentuate the touchiness of a given hull. A lower center of gravity and a relaxed outlook might tame even the most tender of hull designs.

Even with all of these considerations, you can still count on some generalities.

- **Beam.** A boat with a narrower hull may feel sportier and more playful, but this boat might require you to pay more attention to it than wider hull designs. A wider boat will feel very reassuring and will carry more gear, but it might feel sluggish if you are accustomed to quick acceleration and speed.

- **Length.** Longer boats are more efficient cruisers, carry more gear, and track well. However, they are not quick to turn. Shorter boats turn more readily, but they sacrifice the efficiency of the longer waterline.

- **Hard chine versus soft chine.** The chine is the angle of intersection between the hull and the deck. Look at the shoulders, or the sides, of the boat along-

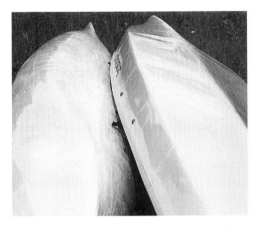

The rounded shoulder of the boat on the left (soft chine) is shown in contrast to the angled departure from hull to deck of the boat on the right (hard chine).

side the cockpit. Do the sides gradually curve upward from the hull to the deck (soft chine)? Or is there an abrupt, almost vertical departure from the hull (hard chine)? The chine of a boat will have a lot to do with how a boat feels on its edge. Soft chine boats have gradual transitions. As you lean a soft chine boat deeper and deeper, it sometimes lacks a point where it will hang with no effort. Hard chine boats have more sudden transitions as you lean them. But on the flat part of the boat's shoulder, you can hang out and carry on a normal conversation with the barest of sculling braces to support you. Traditional Greenland designs have hard chines with a pronounced vee hull. The Inuit-designed *baidarkas* sport multichine hulls.

This discussion of hull design may seem to complicate the picture and make your choice more difficult, but don't let it confuse you. You are not expected to understand hull design after such a short discussion. Entire books have been written on the theory of hull design and how it applies to many types of vessels—from destroyers to kayaks! What you should understand is that kayak hulls are not created equal, and the numbers alone do not describe a boat. You need to sit in a boat, paddle it, lean it, take it out in moderate wind, and then decide if it is the boat for you.

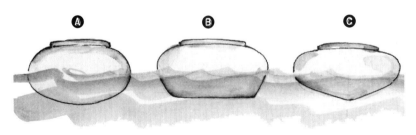

Hull cross sections can tell you a great deal about how the boat will react to waves and how it will feel to the paddler. Waves easily pass under the round-bottom hull **(A)** but it doesn't really care whether it's right side up or upside down. The flat-bottom hull **(B)** tends to be very stable in flat water, but waves cannot readily pass under it. The shallow vee hull **(C)** offers a good combination of seaworthiness, stability, and tracking; a shallow vee or rounded vee is the most common form of sea kayak hull.

CUSTOMIZING YOUR BOAT
• • • • • • • • • • • • • • • • • •

As you spend more time in your boat, you may want to tweak the fit until the boat has the right amount of support and comfort for you. Buy some closed-cell foam (popularly known as mini-cell) in small sheets of 1-inch thickness or less. You can also buy a pre-packaged fit kit, which should be available in your local paddle sports shop. With some waterproof contact cement, a utility knife, Dragonskin mesh, and a Sureform rasp, you are ready to begin work.

First, sit in your boat and decide exactly what you need. With a pencil, outline the areas in your cockpit where you want to add foam. This will give you the general shape and size for the foam pieces. Cut a layer of foam to match these marks. Don't worry about the exact thickness yet. Using duct tape, position these pieces into place.

Next, determine what thickness you need by wedging additional pieces into place until the foam has the desired thickness. You can cut away

continued on page 89

Getting familiar with different hull styles and how they feel on the water is an interesting exercise and another step in your education as a sea kayaker.

Double kayaks

Double kayaks are a great way to travel, especially if there is a disparity in the skill or stamina level of two paddlers who want to travel together. Doubles are also terrific when you add kids and dogs to your paddling plans.

Doubles are very stable. With overall lengths of 18 to 22 feet, they maintain their course well—even in heavy seas. A rudder is useful on a double. In this instance, the rudder is used less for maintaining a course than it is for turning. If both paddlers coordinate their strokes and boat lean, they can turn a double nicely without a rudder. However, on a fully loaded double with large cockpits, leaning the boat isn't that easy. In a double kayak, two paddlers are moving roughly a boat and a half. The speed of a double kayak reflects this.

Double kayaks can cover long distances with little effort and can withstand heavy seas. However, the two paddlers must agree on where to go and cooperate in getting there.

Double kayaks usually have forward and aft storage compartments. Many have large center compartments that can even serve as a third cockpit for a small child. Rudder controls can be attached to the footbraces in either cockpit, though attaching them at the stern position is the most common.

Recreational kayaks

I honestly don't know what to call the kayaks that make great poke-around boats for lakes, ponds, and quiet harbors but are not suitable for open ocean or long distances. A friend calls them "goober boats." The term isn't intended as disrespect—just an easy friendliness!

Recreational models provide stable platforms for lake and protected coastal explorations. They often feature oversized cockpits or a sit-on-top design **(2)** for ease of use.

continued from page 88

areas where the foam is too thick. You can also do some rough carving to get the pieces contoured to your body.

Once you are satisfied with the shape and placement of the foam, glue the pieces into place and let them dry. When it's dry, climb back into your cockpit and use a pencil to mark the areas that need to be smoothed and contoured to finalize the fit. Use the rasp to form the pieces. Then use a piece of Dragonskin mesh (commonly used to finish drywall) to smooth everything and get it exactly right.

These recreational models generally range from 8 to 14 feet in length and are maneuverable and stable. These designs often lack bulkheads (and thus, they lack storage compartments). They are either sit-on-top designs or have oversized cockpits. Large cockpits and the absence of bulkheads is a troubling combination on the open ocean, because your ability to empty your boat of water after a reentry is compromised. In fact, you may not be able to accomplish a solo rescue at all. Sit-on-top designs are fine on the open ocean with their easy reentry (just climb back on), but the shorter lengths and wider hulls that characterize these models make them less efficient for traveling long distances.

These types of boats, however, are great for getting people on the water. The folks that use these boats may never experience the thrill of traveling an open stretch of demanding water or gliding among islands on a multiday adventure, but they will get to enjoy time on the water.

The large majority of recreational kayaks are made of polyethylene, and cost is a major factor in why these boats are so popular. They are scaled down to the essentials (as are the costs). These boats are usually very stable and offer a lot of reassurance. This stability is often a function of a broad, flat bottom that works against you if you paddle in waves. A broad, flat bottom does not readily let waves pass under the hull the way a narrower, vee hull or rounded hull will.

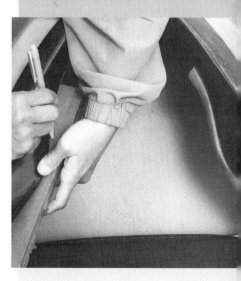

Customize the fit of your boat by attaching foam padding to the underside of the thigh-braces and around the seat. Mark, carve, and attach.

A PRIMER FOR SEA KAYAK BUYERS
• • • • • • • • • • • • • • • • • •

- Don't gather information on every boat and then agonize over the data. It's more important to try boats out on the water.

- Don't delay your choice while you engage in a two-year study of what's available. Get a boat, get on the water, and have a great time. If the relationship fails, it was good while it lasted. Sell that boat and get one that's more your type.

- A 10-minute test paddle on a boat demo day will tell you very little about a given boat. Work with a local paddlesports shop to get more extensive testing or borrow boats from friends or through a local paddling club.

- Your skill level will affect how a boat feels and performs in your hands. While you don't want to buy a boat that is more than you can handle, one that packs some challenge is fun.

continued on page 91

There are times when I prefer to grab my sit-on-top and go surfing or birdwatching in a bog near my home to plying the open waters with my sea kayak. These boats are great fun, and they often lower the perceived barriers that some folks have to getting into a kayak. But don't confuse these boats with the sea kayaks that are designed to weather wind and waves and carry gear for extended travel.

PADDLES

Your paddle is in your hands every time you go kayaking, and your choice of paddle will be as important and personal as your choice of boat. Be willing to spend some money for a decent design so you can enjoy yourself. Paddles range in price from $40 to $350, and they come in a wide variety of shapes and materials. Light weight is a premium; generally, the less a paddle weighs the more it will cost.

When you search for a paddle, use the same approach you would use when looking for your dream boat: Try a variety of paddles and see which feels best to you. Since you should carry a spare paddle, you'll have an opportunity to buy two paddles of very different design and be able to justify your choices with a straight face! Over time, you can find yourself with an entire collection of paddles to fulfill your every whim and use.

Paddle styles

The majority of paddles you find in paddlesports shops have originated from European designs. These paddles have an asymmetric blade that has a spoon shape and a spine up the back side of the blade. They may be made of plastic, plastic-fiber composite, wood, fiberglass, or carbon fiber. It is the combination of these materials that dictates the paddle price; carbon fiber tops the price scale but barely registers on the weight scale. European paddles may be take-apart models with more than one feather angle setting built in, or they may come as one-piece designs. (Feathered paddles are discussed in Chapter 4, "To feather or not to feather," pages 41–42.) Choose a two-piece design for your spare, as it makes on-deck storage easier.

You may also see traditional paddles of Greenland or Inuit design. These paddles are almost always one-piece, unfeathered

Paddles come in many materials and shapes. What a paddle is made of will determine its cost, weight, and durability. The blade design is a matter of personal choice.

continued from page 90

A boat you can grow into as your skills sharpen will be more satisfying in the long run.

- Review your answers to the questions at the beginning of Chapter 2. The boat you choose must match your intended use.

- Make sure the boat is comfortable for you. (I have now said this at least five times. Do you spot a recurring theme?)

- Make sure you can move the boat around on land (you can use a trolley) and get the boat on and off of your car. If you choose a folding or inflatable kayak, make sure you can get it ready to paddle by yourself.

- Don't ignore aesthetics. A boat that you love to look at and show off on top of your car is a boat you will use.

paddles. These traditional paddles usually are crafted in wood and have narrow blades of symmetrical design. They look very different from their European counterparts.

Because of the Greenland or Inuit designs' buoyancy and narrow blades, which are not spooned or asymmetric, many people find it easier to roll and scull with them. With these paddles there is less concern over the blade's tendency to dive, since one face of the blade is the same as the other. The buoyancy of the wood also makes it easy to get the blade to the water's surface. Other paddlers find the buoyancy of these paddles to be distracting; they prefer the greater bite on the water offered by the larger, spooned, European-style blades.

Blade design

Among spooned, asymmetric blades, you will find a variety of blade shapes and sizes. You may notice two blades with very different shapes but with the same square-inch surface area. Those square inches may be packaged in a short, blunt blade shape or spread along a narrower, longer design. Once again, you must look beyond the numbers to find what you like best.

When it comes to overall size, larger blades will give you a greater bite on the water and make it quicker to accelerate your boat. A larger blade also gives you more blade surface during a brace. However, this larger blade surface may feel more sluggish during a sculling brace and may be more fatiguing over the course of a day. Once you are up to cruising speed, it takes very little blade area to maintain your momentum, so blade size is of little consequence during the repetitive strokes used for cruising. Smaller blades offer less wind resistance, and they may tire you less during a long day of paddling.

Paddle length

Once you've chosen your blade design, consider length. Sizing a paddle is not an exact science. Some people agonize over paddle lengths that differ only by 5 centimeters in overall length—that's only about 1 inch per side. Some manufacturers can't even meet this range of accuracy!

A suitable paddle length will allow you to reach the water comfortably without feeling the unwieldiness of unneeded length. Since you should have the entire blade in the water during your forward stroke, blade design will be a factor when deciding on overall length. Some paddlers like a blunt blade design's snappy release from the water; others prefer a longer blade's solid bite and reach.

Shorter, blunter paddle blades will result in shorter overall lengths than long, skinny paddle blades. Consider this: The paddle shaft length might be identical for very different blade designs that differ in overall length by 10 centimeters. Roam around your local paddlesports shop and make these comparisons.

Other factors you should consider when determining paddle length are:

- **The beam of your boat.** A wider boat will require you to have a longer paddle. Know your boat's beam before you go paddle shopping.

- **Your paddling style.** If you use a lot of torso rotation and paddle aggressively you probably will find that you are comfortable with a shorter paddle. A "Sunday driving" style of paddling might require some additional inches in overall length.

Paddle weight

Since you are holding your paddle the entire time you're on the water, paddle weight and balance are critical. Obviously, lighter paddles are less fatiguing over the course of the day. But there is a point of diminishing returns: As a paddle gets lighter, it also becomes more fragile. The weight of a paddle blade in the water is negligible because of its buoyancy, and the weight of the other blade as it swings through the air is perceived to be diminished as it moves forward toward the catch of

"I recommend splurging for a lightweight, carbon fiber paddle. I've seen too many women develop tendinitis—in part because of paddling heavier kayaks, but also because of not having learned proper paddling technique to begin with. Neophytes should get a paddling lesson right away to learn the technique. For those who may have already developed some muscle strain, switch to a lighter paddle."

—Tamsin Venn, kayaking author and publisher of *Atlantic Coastal Kayaker*

the stroke. So, in many ways the "swing weight," or balanced weight, of a paddle is more meaningful than its overall weight. That is why you should try the paddle on the water. But if that isn't possible, at least "air paddle" with it on the sales floor to get a feel for its balance. Hefting a paddle in your hand on a sales floor tells you very little about that paddle.

Make sure you find the grip comfortable. Better models often have the grip positions indexed or made oval for a more comfortable grip. If you choose a take-apart model, make sure you can take it apart and put it back together easily.

Paddle leashes

There will be many times you'll want to set your paddle aside to free both hands. A paddle leash allows you to do this easily. A leash tethers the paddle to either your boat or your wrist. Some leashes are Velcro collars; others are simple loops of line. The most common leashes attach to the forward deck rigging with a plastic clip.

Using a leash has decided advantages. If you drop your paddle or it is blown out of your hands, it is easily retrieved. If you capsize, a paddle tethered to the boat will make both easier to retrieve. Of course, it also lets you lay aside your paddle to put a new roll of film in your camera or add a layer of clothes.

"Lighter is always better! I prefer fiberglass or graphite. . . . And two-piece is always convenient for travel and storage. Since I spend more time in the office than on the water, I usually wear fingerless gloves for protection against blisters."

—Pam Sweeney, manager, Winnipesaukee Kayak Co.

Some paddlers find a long tether to the boat distracting, while others find it reassuring. Tethering a paddle to your wrist might be less distracting as you move through a variety of strokes. However, it won't help you retrieve your boat after a capsize as a paddle-to-boat tether would. Either style must be easily connected and disconnected.

Do not use a paddle leash when surfing. The chance that the line could ensnare you in tumbling surf is too dangerous.

SAFETY EQUIPMENT AND ACCESSORIES

Wearing a life vest is routine safety on a sea kayak, and you already know why you need to carry a paddle float, bilge pump, spare paddle, and rescue sling. These items are essential gear that should travel with you anytime you are on the water. But depending on the conditions, the duration of your trip, and the waters you are paddling in, there are additional pieces of safety equipment that you should consider having onboard.

Rather than making the choice each time I go out, I find it easiest to pack all this gear together in a small mesh duffel and grab it for any trip I take. This approach saves me time, and

I don't get into arguments with myself about whether I really need a piece of safety equipment for a given outing. Better to have it and not need it!

Signaling devices

For any extended open-water paddling, you will need signaling devices—preferably a variety of them. There are a range of audible and visual devices used by paddlers.

Signaling by sound

The easiest and cheapest device you can carry is a rescue whistle. This will last far longer and carry much farther than your voice. These whistles can be attached to the zipper tab of your life vest. That way, you will automatically have your whistle every time you go boating. And if you are bobbing in the water, the whistle will float close to your mouth.

The "pealess" plastic whistles are best. They won't clog in sticky saltwater environments. You may use a whistle in non-emergency situations as well. For example, you might create a system of simple signals that you can use for group communication.

If you paddle in low-visibility conditions, carry a foghorn as another sound signal. When you find yourself paddling in the fog among boat traffic, use your foghorn to signal at least every two minutes. Then listen for any signals from nearby boats. Learning other vessels' fog signals is worthwhile if you paddle in an area where fog is prevalent. You can also use a foghorn in clear visibility to signal other vessels if you have a problem or to avoid a collision. I recommend using a foghorn you can blow rather than one that depends on a pressurized pack. There's less chance of a malfunction or of simply running out of canister pressure. Always make sure your foghorn is working before you launch.

Visual signaling devices

Visual signaling devices are crucial in the event of an emergency. Getting the attention of anyone nearby or marking your location for vessels coming to your aid must be done quickly and efficiently.

Waving a paddle overhead with the blade held high is a useful signal, but it works only in fairly close quarters. For longer-range signaling, small handheld aerial flares (orange) send their signals as high as 500 feet. Most paddlesports shops sell these flares in packs of three (I suggest you carry more than one pack). These flares fit easily inside your life vest pocket. Their visibility is pretty puny on the open ocean, but they can be seen from a reasonable distance for coastal and lake paddlers.

If you plan to paddle regularly on open water well offshore, I recommend investing in some parachute flares or in a flare pistol. Both are significantly more powerful than the small, handheld versions. They are more expensive, but they have the firepower to send brighter signals higher. You can also purchase flares that can be ignited and held or attached to the boat to mark your location.

Orange smoke canisters are easy to carry in a pocket, and they give off a bright orange smoke that is surprisingly effective—even in breezy conditions. (Remember, though, that these will dissi-

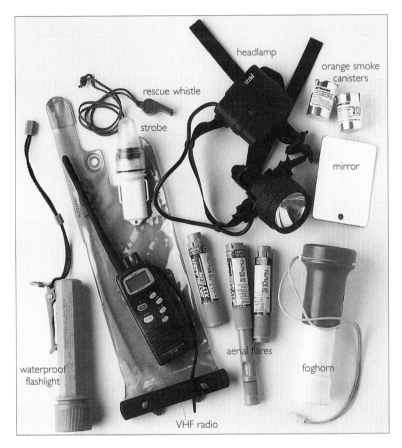

Signaling devices aboard your kayak should include visual and sound signals and nighttime as well as daytime signals. A VHF radio and cellular phone provide communication links in case of emergency.

PADDLING AT NIGHT

There's nothing quite as magical as paddling under a full moon. Everything is bathed in silver, and you feel as if you have a special porthole onto the world.

If you paddle at night, make sure every boat in the group has a flashlight or head-lamp. It's also a good idea to equip everyone with a cyalume glowstick so every member of the group can be kept in sight. Group leaders should pack flares, and before launching you should discuss as a group the whistle signals you will use. "Buddy up" during nighttime paddles; you'll be ready to respond quickly if necessary, and it's just kind of nice to know someone is watching out for you if the moon ducks behind a cloud.

pate faster in wind.) Smoke canisters should include a note stating their activity duration; it usually ranges from 30 to 60 seconds. Be careful to store these in their original shrink-wrap or in a zip-top bag. A leaky canister can make a real mess of your gear.

A small signaling mirror is useful on sunny days. You can direct it at another vessel for effective signaling in emergencies. A strobe worn on your life vest shoulder is a smart addition for nighttime paddling. Make sure to regularly check batteries, grease the gasket, and clean the contacts.

Since you probably pack a headlamp or flashlight for any overnight trip, make it a waterproof one and store it in an accessible spot as dusk approaches. To meet inland and international navigation rules, you are required to carry a white light ready to

> "I carry flares and, thank goodness, have *never* had to use them in the 30 years I've been paddling. Does that say something for my common sense?"
>
> —Judy Moyer, co-owner,
> Pacific Water Sports

be displayed in time to prevent collision if you paddle between dusk and dawn on most waters. You can stick a flashlight under your deck rigging for a running light. Or use a headlamp, which will free your hands and allow you to direct your beam of light with a turn of your head. (I have one tip regarding your light: In some areas, your light beam will draw insects—so you might want to disassociate yourself from it. I've had bats bump the side of my boat as they fed on these insects. Better the boat than the side of my head!)

A word about signaling devices

Signaling devices—with the exception of your whistle and flashlight—are meant to be used for specific signaling or emergency purposes. Under no circumstances should you use a flare or smoke canister unless you need immediate assistance. These are irreversible signals indicating an emergency. Remember to carry a variety of signaling devices that will cover you in a range of light conditions, from full sun to dark, and make sure you strike a balance between the visual and sound devices you carry onboard.

Check your signaling equipment regularly. Since you don't use these devices each time you go out, it is easy to forget about this task. Make sure your gear is kept clean and in good working order. Check that all your flares are within their expiration date. You can keep your old flares as spares in your boat—but don't count on them to work when needed.

Radios and cell phones

VHF radios and cellular phones provide you the means to signal for help, and they also allow you to relay information to an outside party about your situation and your location.

VHF radios, a means of onboard communication used by mariners and ships, have different channels you can use for communication. Certain channels are continually monitored by the U.S. Coast Guard and other mariners. On these channels, there is always a party listening in case of an emergency. Other channels are for ship-to-ship communication and for accessing local marine operators to place calls ashore. You can also monitor weather reports by the National Oceanic and Atmospheric Administration (NOAA) over your VHF. Reports for specific coastal and offshore zones are given around the clock. On longer trips, you will want to carry a weather radio as well so you can save your VHF batteries (usually expensive nickel-cadmium packs) for communication. There is a protocol to using VHF radios, which may be provided with your radio. You can also contact your local Coast Guard Station or Coast Guard Auxiliary for information about protocol and to find out what channel(s) they monitor regularly.

Over the years VHF radios have gotten smaller and less expensive. Handheld versions are available for $150 to $500. Some claim to be waterproof; while their electronics may be, the battery packs are notorious for failing due to corrosion.

Cellular phones are easily packed for a trip. In most coastal waters, cellular phones provide reliable reception since your line of sight from the water to a coastal tower is usually good. A cellular phone will put you in touch with emergency services quickly, but it will not provide communication lines to other nearby vessels or to weather information like a VHF will. VHF radios and cellular phones—even "waterproof versions"—must be stored in waterproof bags or containers, along with spare batteries.

Life vests (personal flotation devices)

The days of uncomfortable horse-collar life vests are gone—so you have absolutely no excuse for not wearing your life vest at all times. Most kayakers wear a Type III vest designed for canoeing and kayaking. The cut is short so the vest doesn't ride up when you're in a seated paddling position, and the good ones are sized to fit with additional compression straps for fine-tuning.

Several companies are now manufacturing life vests for women, and some are getting rave reviews—especially from women with larger breasts who found the unisex styles a poor fit.

Life vests should be brightly colored or at least adorned with bright tape patches for good visibility. Consider adding pieces of retroreflective tape to the top of the shoulders and upper back for increased visibility at night. Retroreflective tape comes in several colors, but silver is the most common, and it's available by the foot or in pre-cut patches. You will find it at your local paddlesports shop or marine store.

Always wear your life vest and keep it zipped. Storing your vest behind your seat and assuming you can slip it on if you capsize or get into trouble is just plain stupid.

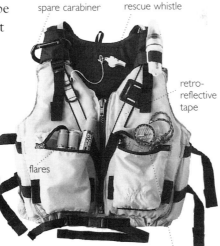

spare carabiner   rescue whistle

retro-reflective tape

flares

handheld compass

Your life vest should be highly visible and should be adjustable for a snug fit all around. Signaling devices and small pieces of gear can be carried on or in your life vest.

Many life vests are designed with pockets and attachment points so you can carry signaling devices and other equipment such as towlines. You may feel a bit like Rambo with all this gear rattling around on you. But if you are paddling in remote and challenging areas, there is an advantage to having this gear accessible at all times.

Sprayskirts

In open water and rough conditions, sprayskirts are safety equipment because they keep wave slosh and water out of your boat. In less extreme conditions, sprayskirts protect your legs from sun (and funny tan lines) and the slow torture of paddle drips in your lap with each stroke.

Sprayskirts can be made of nylon or neoprene or a combination of the two materials. Nylon skirts generally have a looser fit and are cooler in warm weather. But nylon sprayskirts do not keep out serious wave action, and they are not recommended for surfing or other more challenging outings—especially those that might involve rolling. Neoprene will keep you warmer and drier, but a neoprene sprayskirt may be too warm for a typical summertime paddle.

Towlines

Towlines are invaluable when someone is ill or injured far from shore or if you need to retrieve a wayward boat. Towing can also provide an easy boost for an exhausted paddler or help pace a weak paddler in a group.

Pack a towline for any group outing; larger groups should carry several (a 1:3 ratio is typical). A towline suitable for sea kayaking consists of 25 to 30 feet of floating line (usually 1/4- to 5/16-inch polypropylene) with an anodized carabiner on one end. This carabiner clips onto the boat being towed, usually through the bow toggle.

The towline packs into a small bag worn around your waist or mounted on deck. The bag includes a quick-release mechanism that allows you to drop the towline easily with one hand. You can also incorporate a piece of bungee into the base of a towline to help smooth out yanks and jolts to the towing

KINDER, GENTLER TOWING
•••••••••••••••••••••

Unfortunately, there has always been a stigma attached to being towed. Occasionally, those needing a tow have been pegged as weak or inadequate and have even been made to feel unwelcome on a paddling outing. Many paddlers have plugged along in a near-exhausted state rather than accept a tow—and the reproach attached when that carabiner snaps into place. Of course, this is a dangerous attitude on the parts of both the paddler needing a tow and those coming to her aid.

A towline is useful in far less extreme cases. It can help pace a slow paddler on a long crossing when keeping the group together is essential. It can slow down an aggressive paddler champing at the bit. Or it can be used to "buddy up" boats in poor visibility or on long open stretches. Pairing up boats with towlines lets everyone work at their own pace, much the way a double kayak or canoe does.

Towing isn't just for the weak or injured. It should be considered a tool for group management on the water.

paddler. Towlines are available from many manufacturers, with prices starting at around $25.

Most towing paddlers find it easiest to wear the towline around their waist on a quick-release nylon belt, much like the belts used in scuba diving. Wearing it there keeps the pull of towing centered on your boat, provides continuous feedback throughout the tow, and raises the line enough to clear any rudder mechanisms.

A word of caution about towing: You should practice employing a towline and releasing it from your waist before attempting to use it in a real situation. Practice releasing the towline while you are upright and then with your boat overturned to ensure you can free yourself when needed. There is a responsibility that comes with wearing a towline. Before launching, groups should discuss who will be wearing towlines.

CLOTHING AS SAFETY GEAR

To be adequately protected from the elements means investing in some decent paddlesports clothing. I am not talking fashion here. But you do need the right stuff: materials that will protect you from wind, water, cold, heat, and sun—and continue to protect you even if you are immersed in the water.

Cold water protection and hypothermia

Unless you are lucky enough to paddle year round in toasty water and air temperatures, you need to be aware of hypothermia—the gravest danger to most sea kayakers. Hypothermia occurs when your body temperature drops below normal. Early stages of hypothermia may produce shivering, clumsiness, and a general lethargy. Advanced stages result in unconsciousness and can even lead to death.

Having been moderately hypothermic more than once, I can tell you that it is frightening. Your manual dexterity is gone; you become clumsy and confused; you stop making sound decisions. For sea kayakers, this situation is particularly frightening: Without our balance, dexterity, and the ability to make sound decisions, we are truly helpless.

To recover from hypothermia requires getting dry and warm, a feat not easily accomplished in your boat on the water. That is why *preventing* hypothermia is extremely important for all paddlers.

Immersion in water will cool your body at least 25 percent faster, through conductive cooling, than the same air temperature. And just getting out of the water isn't enough. A wet body exposed to a breeze will chill rapidly due to evaporative cooling across the surface of your skin. You must be prepared for these events every time you go paddling. To ignore the possibility of getting wet is foolish.

When you go paddling, assume you will get wet and you may be immersed in the water. Be prepared with your clothing and skills. A warm, sunny day coupled with cold water is when we usually make poor decisions as paddlers. We may dress for the balmy air temperature only to be stunned by the cold water. If you are prepared for the water temperature, you will be safe. You might get steamy in your cockpit as you swelter in a wetsuit. But you are surrounded by all that cold water, so it's pretty easy to cool off. Dip a hat or bandanna over the side, have a bilge-pump water fight, or practice your roll or reentry techniques.

Sea kayaking students often ask for a hard and fast water temperature that acts as a magic cut-off point: Above it you can wear anything you want; below it requires a wetsuit or drysuit. But it isn't that simple.

You need to factor many variables into your decision. How likely is immersion? (With surfing it's a sure bet.) How solid are your boating skills (especially rolling and solo reentry) and your balance and comfort level in your boat? Are there aggravating factors such as wind? How accessible is the shore and what does it offer if you need to warm up? Who are your paddling partners, how prepared are they, and how strong are your skills in relation to theirs? (Are they expecting *you* to take care of *them*?) After all that, what I will give you is a rough guideline: Except in benign and fully protected paddling conditions, you should wear either a wetsuit or a drysuit with proper layering in water temperatures of 60°F (16°C) or colder. Pack a thermos of something hot and sweet (cocoa or sugared coffee) for a quick boost of energy and warmth.

Any fabrics you wear on the water must be quick to dry, and they must continue to warm you even when wet. Synthetic fabrics such as pile or fleece work well. Wool will continue to warm you when wet but it grows heavy in the water and is much slower to dry. Never wear cotton clothing on the water; it gets heavy when wet and will pull heat from

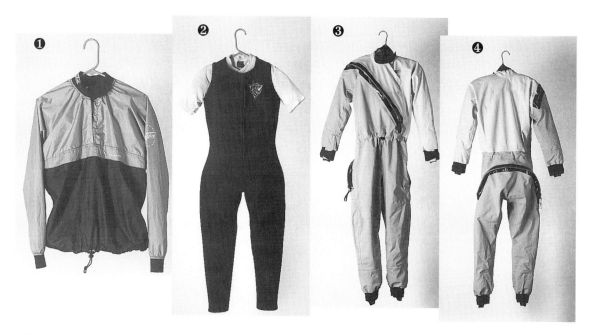

1. A paddling jacket provides a windproof and waterproof outer layer. **2.** Farmer Jane/John wetsuits are the most popular cold-water clothing. A synthetic shirt worn underneath can prevent chafing and help keep you warm when wet. **3.** If you regularly paddle in cold water, a drysuit is an excellent choice. The Gore-Tex version is a luxury you'll never regret. **4.** Drysuits aren't easy to take on and off quickly. A drop-seat option is a useful feature for women paddlers.

your body through evaporative cooling, creating a dangerous situation.

Your outer layers should be waterproof and provide you with wind protection. The layers next to your body should wick moisture away from your skin and provide warmth. Synthetic thermal underwear is the best thing to wear next to your body in cold water situations. Don't forget to wear a hat to prevent heat loss from your head. Consider neoprene paddling gloves or pogies (paddling mitts that attach to the paddle shaft) for your hands and neoprene booties for your feet.

Wetsuits and drysuits

A wetsuit is made of neoprene, a closed-cell material that insulates your body by trapping a thin layer of water next to your skin. This water is warmed by your body, and it will buy you time if you are immersed in cold water. Your wetsuit must fit snugly. Otherwise, water will simply flush through and leave you chilled. If you are immersed for any length of time, it helps to pee in your wetsuit (an old scuba diving trick). This may sound uncouth, but it works like a charm if you need a quick warmup. You can rinse everything later.

Paddlers usually find the Farmer Jane/John–style wetsuit to be the most comfortable. Prices start around $95. This type of wetsuit is sleeveless with a long front-entry zipper, and it comes in full- or short-leg lengths. Most paddling wetsuits are 2 to 3 millimeters in thickness. Anything thicker is too restrictive and uncomfortable for most paddling. With a wetsuit, you still need a windproof layer on top, especially for your upper body. A paddling jacket, nylon parka, or anorak works well.

Although significantly more expensive than a wetsuit, a drysuit is a great choice for cold-water paddling. Drysuits keep you totally dry inside—even if you have to go swimming. A drysuit is a suit of waterproof fabric closed off with latex gaskets at the neck, ankles, and wrists that seal the suit and keep water out. These latex gaskets are thin and lie flat on your skin (baby powder is a must), and the suit is closed with a waterproof zipper.

You may begin to feel like a boiled turnip inside your drysuit—and smell like one when you unzip it! If you use a

A WATER BOTTLE AS SAFETY EQUIPMENT

Sea kayakers are notorious for dehydrating themselves while paddling. The idea of making multiple pit stops prevents many paddlers from consuming sufficient liquids while they are on the water (see Chapter 9, "To pee or not to pee," page 148). This is a dangerous scenario anytime, but it is especially dangerous in hot climates. The onset of a headache is a sure sign that you are behind in your fluid consumption. It is your body's way of telling you to reach for the water bottle.

Having plenty of water onboard is part of being a safety-conscious paddler. You can stick water bottles on deck, behind your seat, or in a day hatch, if one is available. In hot climates, store a bottle inside your boat; it will stay cooler there and gain refrigeration through the hull from the water temperature. You can also opt to wear a hydration system on your back or use one in a deck bag. That way, your hands will be free to paddle at all times.

CONTACT LENSES
• • • • • • • • • • • • • • • • • •

You certainly can wear your contact lenses while paddling, but you probably will appreciate a pair of sunglasses on top. Salt water can really sting if it gets in your eyes, and a wave hitting your face can actually wash your lenses away. (I once retrieved a lens from the shoulder of my life vest and had to pop it in my mouth for safekeeping until I got to shore.)

Consider wearing wraparound sunglasses or adding side pieces to your frames for additional wind and water protection. I found that regular sunglass frames often funneled wind into the sides of my eyes and then folded over my soft contact lenses. Clipping on side pieces solved the problem.

Make sure to pack a mirror, lots of extra saline, and an extra set of lenses or glasses when you're paddling, especially on multiday trips. Remember to rinse salt from your hands before handling your lenses.

drysuit regularly, you won't hesitate to spring for the expensive Gore-Tex version ($600 and up) that is breathable.

You should wear whatever layers you need to keep warm inside your drysuit. You'll stay dry, but remember that you'll still feel the cold of the water if you are immersed wearing a drysuit.

Waterproof bags (drybags)

Keeping gear and extra clothing dry while paddling is a must. No hatch system, regardless of manufacturers' claims, should be trusted to keep your stuff bone dry. You'll need drybags for that.

Drybags come in all sizes, shapes, and colors. Most have some type of roll-down closure that is then snapped or buckled closed. Drybags usually are made of vinyl or coated nylon, and all seams are welded for waterproofing. Nylon bags slide more easily in and out of kayak hatches but are slightly more expensive than vinyl ones. Since drybags come in many shapes, you can maximize the amount of gear (and bags) you can fit in your kayak's storage compartments.

Rigid waterproof cases are less useful than drybags since they can't be compressed to fit around other gear and often won't fit through hatch openings. But if you carry expensive camera equipment, you will need a container that is both water- and shock-proof. These rigid cases offer both. They have a gasket around the lip of the case to seal out water, and they usually come with interior foam layers that you can shape to fit your gear.

Protection from the sun

Your boat may protect your lower body from the sun's rays. But you will still need lots of protection from the sun for the rest of your body. Lightweight clothing and sunscreen can offer you respite from the sun. Get a well ventilated hat with floppy sides to protect the tops of your ears and the back of your neck. Many paddlers forget that glare from the water will burn them underneath the shade of a hat's brim: Don't forget sunscreen on your face, the tops of your ears, and your neck—even if you wear a hat with a wide brim.

Your sunscreen should be SPF 15 or greater, and you should apply it liberally throughout the day. A waterproof variety works best, for obvious reasons. Avoid getting any on your palms and your paddle shaft, which makes a slippery mess. Protect your lips with a good lip balm and wear sunglasses for UV protection of your eyes. Look for sunglasses that offer both UV-A and UV-B protection, and consider polarized lenses for the best glare protection. You'll need a retainer strap for your eyewear.

CARE AND FEEDING FOR EQUIPMENT

There is very little maintenance required of sea kayakers. Having a routine of washing and inspecting your gear each time you go paddling is the best preventive maintenance.

Checking your equipment before and after each use will help you prevent a minor tear or ding from becoming a full-scale repair job. Wash out your gear and allow it to dry before storing it away. Use a hose nozzle to flush sand and grunge from your footbraces, the joints of a folding boat, and the top of your car. (Saltwater drips are deadly over time.)

You also need to take steps against the sun's potential damage of your equipment and learn how to properly stow your gear.

Sunscreen for equipment

You can spray or wipe a product called 303 Protectant on your equipment to protect it from UV degradation. It protects boats and prevents their fading, keeps latex drysuit gaskets supple and less prone to tearing, and even keeps chart cases and rubber hatch covers from becoming brittle and chalky. Use this product at least several times a year for general maintenance. If you're the type who tends to wax her car often, you might feel better using 303 Protectant more often. (Composite boats can be waxed too, but waxes don't provide as much UV resistance.)

Proper storage

Store your gear out of direct sunlight in a well ventilated area so mildew will not degrade any fabric pieces. Your boat should be supported on its side (at the bulkhead positions) or slung with overhead support around these areas. Never hang your boat by the carrying toggles alone: Polyethylene boats will sag, and you will stress the anchor eyelets on composite boats. If you leave your polyethylene boat with its hull flat on the ground or a rack, its surface will eventually dimple or droop, leaving you with a less efficient hull for paddling.

If you must store gear for long periods, use a cockpit cover to keep out insects and rodents. Check your stored gear regularly for any signs of animal

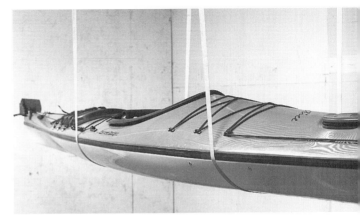

Support your boat as close to the bulkheads as possible. A set of webbing slings in a garage works well and may be useful for solo loading on your car.

damage (a porcupine once destroyed my seat). When you remove your gear from long-term storage, make sure you check the cockpit for insect nests before hopping back in. Trust me, you'll only forget to do this once!

The perils of car-topping

If you carry your boat on top of your car for prolonged periods of time, make sure the cockpit or hatches have not taken on water. A cockpit full of water and a jolting bump are a recipe for fractures to composite boats and will cause a polyethylene boat to sag. Use a cockpit cover to keep water and any ugly, crawly things out of your boat. Check your straps and lines to ensure they are not overtightened and are not caught on fragile edges, such as your cockpit coaming. If you leave your boat strapped into place on your car for long periods of time, you may find that your boat has developed tan lines where the straps crossed the deck. You may also see rubs from strap buckles and sand or grit caught under the webbing. Prevent this by running the webbing through your hand to knock off harmful grit before strapping down your boat.

Paddles

Store two-piece paddles in separate pieces. Position the openings pointing down so any water that might have accumulated in the shaft can drain out. Clean the joints on two-piece paddles both inside and out with a bottle brush and wash with fresh water. Never spray or coat these areas with wet lubricants. These lubricants will attract grit and dust particles and actually hold the pieces in place. If you have a hard time working with the joint on your two-piece paddle, you can use dry graphite to dust the joint and make it easier to use. Over time the joint will wear down (especially on carbon fiber versions) and develop some play, so you don't want to do anything to accelerate this process.

One-piece paddles can hang on a wall much like your garden tools. Or you can stand them in a corner. Don't store any paddles—especially wooden ones—next to a furnace or wood stove. When retrieving them from storage, check wooden paddles for cracks or delamination; you may need to reglue a separated section or coat the paddle with a layer of varnish or oil. Check the manufacturer's recommendations first.

Drysuits and wetsuits

Before storing drysuits and wetsuits, always wash them and allow them to dry. Use a mild dilute detergent or wetsuit shampoo and rinse thoroughly. Never store wetsuits or neoprene sprayskirts in a folded position. You will create creases in the material that are very hard to remove. Drysuit gaskets should be regularly coated with 303 Protectant, allowed to dry, and then dusted with baby powder before storing. Never store paddling clothing, sprayskirts, or life vests until they are dry.

At some point you will need to replenish the waterproof treatment on your paddling jacket or drysuit. There are products, such as those by Nikwax, that can do this during a normal washing machine cycle for both non-breathable and breathable fabrics. Consult individual manufacturers for guidance on more detailed repairs to fabrics and gaskets.

Minor boat repairs

Over time your kayak will probably develop a variety of dings, dents, and scratches—all signs of your enjoyment! If these bother you, there are ways to make most of them disappear. If your boat develops a major problem (sizable holes through the cloth; large fractured areas or soft spots), consider contacting your local paddlesports shop or marina for repairs. Large-scale repairs aren't much fun and can be difficult to hide. It might be best to hire someone to do the job.

Composite boat repair

You can make most surface scratches and nicks disappear by buffing your boat with a fine rubbing compound, available at most hardware or auto parts stores. Use a soft cloth or a buffing wheel (a soft, fuzzy disc attachment for your power drill) and a light touch.

A deeper gouge, where gelcoat has actually been chipped from the surface, requires a gelcoat patch. Most manufacturers sell matching gelcoat colors, which make repairs barely noticeable. The shelf life of gelcoat and its catalytic hardener is no more than one boating season. If you have only minor chips, you might consider ignoring the repair or covering them with duct tape. Another option is to coordinate the repair with other paddlers or with a local shop. It breaks my heart to throw away cans of unusable gelcoat each season—the stuff is nasty and toxic.

Since the catalytic hardener that goes with your gelcoat requires special permits and shipping, most manufacturers are unable to ship it to you. Luckily, you can find the hardener at an auto parts store or a marine chandlery.

Following are the basic steps of a gelcoat repair:

- **Protect yourself.** Any use of acetone and gelcoat repair materials must be done in a well ventilated area away from any open flames. You must wear latex gloves, a respirator, and protection for your eyes at all times.

- **Prep the damaged area.** Before you begin a gelcoat repair, use masking tape to mask off the repair area to protect against scratching and clean the wound with acetone. If there are jagged edges, bevel them and smooth them out with some wet/dry sandpaper. Remove any loose bits of gelcoat.

1. Masking tape can protect the area around the repair from scratching and gelcoat drips.

- **Apply the gelcoat.** Mix gelcoat with a few drops of hardener. (Check directions provided by the manufacturer for specific instructions.) Quickly work the gelcoat into place and leave it just proud of (just above) the surface and smoothed out from the edges. Cover the patch with waxed paper and clean the area outside of the patch with acetone. The patch should set for several hours until it is completely dry and hard.

2. Once you've added the hardener to the gelcoat, smooth the repair quickly, before the material hardens.

- **The final steps.** Remove the waxed paper and wet-sand the repair with 320-grit wet/dry sandpaper until the repaired area is almost level with the surrounding area. Finish off with 600-grit wet/dry sandpaper and plenty of water. You may buff out any edge scratches that may have occurred with rubbing compound.

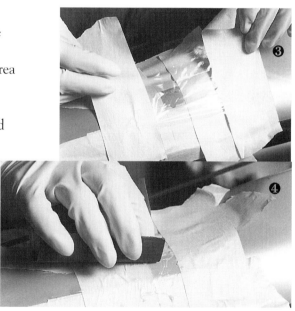

3. Cover the repair with plastic wrap or wax paper and allow it to dry.
4. Wet-sand with progressively finer paper to smooth the repair and blend it with the surrounding area.

When you do a gelcoat repair, make sure you have everything close at hand and that you won't be interrupted. The repair material sets up quickly, so you must be organized and ready to go. If the damaged area has white, spiderweb-shaped lines in the cloth and surrounding resin, the damage is of a structural nature and the repair is more involved. You can look at the damaged area from the inside of your boat for these telltale signs. Structural repairs are best done by a local shop that has repair experience. The materials are nasty, and getting it right the first time is not guaranteed. If you prefer to do structural repairs yourself, contact your boat's manufacturer for information. For more detailed boat repair instructions and other great gear maintenance tips, check out Annie Getchell's *Essential Outdoor Gear Manual*.

Polyethylene boat repair

The most common repairs done on polyethylene boats are the removal of dents and dimples and resealing the bulkheads.

Dents and dimples can be removed with gentle heat and pressure. Polyethylene does have a type of "memory," and often you can get the dimpled area to pop back out by putting the boat out in the sun with the area exposed. You can help this process along by putting a tire inner tube inside the boat and inflating it. This will help push the area out from the inside.

Some dents demand more aggressive heating, which can be done with an industrial hair dryer. You must continually move the heat source and check to make sure the area isn't becoming soft by overheating. A hair dryer also works well on all the little curls and edges that develop from hull abuse. These can also be trimmed with a sharp putty knife or ski wax scraper.

It is unlikely that your polyethylene boat will be punctured or cracked. If you somehow manage this, your boat will need to be plastic welded. Plastic welding isn't difficult to do, but it is tricky to do correctly without causing even more structural damage to the boat. Overheating the area is one potential risk. Be extremely careful if you choose to attempt this type of repair. In fact, the very presence of a crack or puncture should make you wonder if your boat is ready for retirement. As polyethylene ages it becomes more brittle and more prone to damage, especially when it is cold. If your

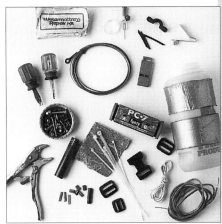

A useful array of tools, repair parts, and materials can be stored in a wide-mouth bottle and taken along on every paddling trip.

A BOAT REPAIR KIT

There are a few odds and ends you might need for a quick boat repair during a trip. You should create your own repair kit that includes parts specific to your equipment—and don't forget the duct tape! The following can be stored in a 1-quart Nalgene wide-mouth bottle and thrown in a hatch on every trip. Your duct tape can be wound around the outside. That way, it doesn't take any additional space and is right there with your repair kit at all times.

Handy sea kayak repair kit

- 4-inch Vise-Grip pliers
- stainless steel machine screws (in all sizes your equipment uses)
- locknuts (in all sizes your equipment uses)
- an extra rudder or skeg cable
- a handful of wire cable swages for crimping cables
- a mini-screwdriver (flat, Phillips head, or both—depending on your gear)
- a lighter for sealing ends of bungee or nylon line
- several gear eyes (the eyes on deck that the rigging is laced through)
- rudder track screws with O-rings
- replacement buckles and ladder-locks for hatch straps
- wire ties and shrink tubing
- a small tube of contact cement
- vinyl repair kit for dry bags, air mattresses, flotation bags
- two-part epoxy putty
- eyeglass repair kit
- various pieces of small line
- spring button for take-apart paddle

boat has been around for 5 or more years *and* is very faded, it might be time to send it to the recycling bin. (Ask the manufacturer or your local transfer station if they will accept it for recycling.)

For plastic welding, you will need to get some matching color scraps from your boat's manufacturer to get a reasonably close match in color. If you don't want to wait, you can use P-Tex, a ski-base repair material. Either material can be welded into the damaged area, although you can rarely make a polyethylene weld disappear.

Since polyethylene expands and contracts as the temperature changes, the sealant around the bulkheads has the tough job of staying flexible and in place. Inspect the bead of sealant on both sides of the bulkheads for cracks or gaps on a regular basis. If you find areas where the sealant is loose, you will need to reseal the bulkhead with a high-quality marine sealant. Among the brands that can be used are Sikaflex, Kop-R-lastic, and Lexel. Check the owner's manual for your kayak. It may recommend a specific brand.

To do a plastic welding repair, you will need to know what kind of polyethylene your boat is made of. If you don't know, start by contacting the shop where you bought it, and call the manufacturer if necessary. Some types of polyethylene, such as cross-link polyethylene, cannot be repaired by plastic welding methods at home (they also cannot be recycled). Linear polyethylene, the most common type used in kayaks, is weldable. Read through the following steps to decide if you really want to tackle this project.

- **Clean the area.** Use a soft cloth and alcohol, and remove any curls or plastic or dirt from around the wound.

- **Warm the area.** Gently warm the area around the opening using a hair dryer. This warming readies the area to accept the repair material. The surface should not bubble or turn dark.

- **Prepare the repair material.** Hold your matching color chip of polyethylene or P-Tex over the wound (wearing a pair of insulated gloves) and heat the chip until it is soft and ready to drip into the wound.

- **Apply repair material.** Hold the dripping repair material over the wound and drip or rub until the area is filled. It is extremely important that you heat only the repair material, not the boat material.

- **Smooth the repair.** Use the back of a kitchen spoon to smooth the area, and then let it set up.

- **Check your work.** Make sure the repair is complete. You may need to add additional material.

Chapter 7

PUTTING IT ALL TOGETHER

Being out there is what it's all about: dealing with wind, waves, weather, and the personality of your boat. I call this the "Aha!" chapter due to my satisfied muttering when I finally worked through these strategies, many times with blessed guidance. But don't take my word for it. Experience the passing of a cold front. Let the wind blow you around and figure out why. Watch the water change texture and direction at the edge of a river mouth as a tidal current plays tug of war with the wind. Then come back and see if I got it right.

STAYING ON COURSE

When you use your boat for traveling, you want to paddle a given course and waste as little energy as possible. The quickest way to waste energy is to lose your forward momentum. Novice paddlers often do this—they get too far off course and then have to stop and bring their boat back on line. To avoid this "snake-wake" style of paddling, you must monitor your boat's course and progress.

Get used to looking ahead at an object or series of objects to gauge your kayak's position. If your boat strays off course, you can detect this early on and react accordingly. Bringing your boat back on course without losing forward momentum requires nothing more than shifting your weight in the cockpit.

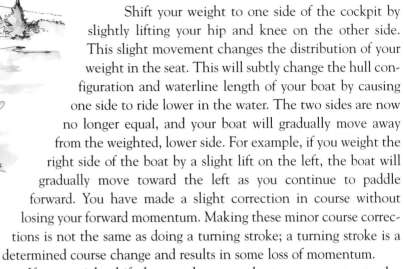

Shift your weight to one side of the cockpit by slightly lifting your hip and knee on the other side. This slight movement changes the distribution of your weight in the seat. This will subtly change the hull configuration and waterline length of your boat by causing one side to ride lower in the water. The two sides are now no longer equal, and your boat will gradually move away from the weighted, lower side. For example, if you weight the right side of the boat by a slight lift on the left, the boat will gradually move toward the left as you continue to paddle forward. You have made a slight correction in course without losing your forward momentum. Making these minor course corrections is not the same as doing a turning stroke; a turning stroke is a determined course change and results in some loss of momentum.

If your weight shift does not keep your boat on course, try to also adjust your forward stroke on the weighted side. Reach out farther with more of a sweeping motion to accentuate your course correction without losing momentum.

Look ahead to landmarks as you paddle. Make minor course corrections by shifting your weight in the cockpit while continuing to paddle forward.

The idea behind these subtle course corrections is to avoid wasting energy. Your strokes should be continuous and smooth, and your weight shift should become second nature as you respond to your boat's movement through the water. It's like climbing a set of stairs: Your body makes a constant appraisal of stair height and depth so you can place your foot in the right spot. Building these subtle techniques into your everyday paddling puts you in firm control of your boat. It transforms what could be a struggle into a confident day on the water.

WAVES

Most of the waves you encounter will be born from the wind. As the wind begins to blow, the water begins to show signs of choppiness. As the wind strengthens, white caps become visible. With even stronger winds, signs of streaking and spray will appear. As the wind blows harder, waves will grow in height and may begin to break on themselves—even in deep water. A basic understanding of how waves are created and diminished is useful.

The height of a wind-created wave is determined by three factors: (1) the velocity of the wind; (2) the duration of that wind; and (3) the fetch (or unimpeded distance) that wind has traveled over the water. Knowing these three factors will allow you to make certain predictions about local paddling conditions.

For example, you know that an island-studded coastline (*i.e.*, one with a short fetch) will never have large waves in its inner passage the way a coastline exposed to open ocean (*i.e.*, a long

• •

" . . . I would go out on a day when the waves were puny and then tell myself—yes, this I can do. Then I'd go out on a day when the waves were slightly bigger and try to relax and get used to being out there. Once I was a little impatient with myself and I kept threatening myself that I wasn't going to take myself back to shore until I calmed down and felt comfortable in those conditions. It didn't take too long (thank goodness) and I was comfortable enough to return to the beach."

—Linda Legg, kayak instructor and guide

• •

fetch) will. That is one reason why surfers congregate in Hawaii and parts of California and shun Maine.

There are other factors in wave formation. Storms at sea and seismic events beneath the ocean may create waves or long swells that are outside your ability to predict. But knowing these three components of wind-driven waves will help you make some general predictions.

Topography and waves

Waves will also be affected by the topography they travel over. When moving water encounters the additional drag created by a shallow bottom, water begins piling up on itself as the bottom layers are slowed and the faster-moving top layers begin to spill. A gradually sloping bottom allows the wave to gently release its energy by spilling onto the beach. If the bottom rises sharply and

WAVE HEIGHT

• • • • • • • • • • • • • • • • •

As you sit in your kayak on the water, it doesn't take much of a wave to block your view. Waves viewed from a kayak look imposing, and it's very tempting to think the waves over our heads are 6, 12, even 18 feet high! In reality, that wave may be only 30 inches high. When you're seated in a kayak, your eye level is only about 26 to 30 inches off the water; that towering wall of water descending on you may pack embarrassingly small statistics.

Paddling in deep-water waves is a lot of fun. Your boat rises to great heights on a crest and descends out of sight in a trough. I was leading a group of novice kayakers through a deep-water channel outside an island's edge, enjoying the heady lifts of a sizable swell and even the anxious

continued on page 112

It's easy to misjudge wave height when your eyes are only 26 to 30 inches above the water.

continued from page 111

moment of losing sight of my ducklings in the trough. (You learn to count heads very quickly.) A nearby lighthouse 100 feet or so above the water disappeared with each drop into the trough. At lunch break, my students were exhilarated as they talked about their "elevator rides" by kayak. They wanted to know exactly how high those waves were. Student estimates ranged from a minimum of 20 feet to a maximum of 110 feet. (The latter figure was blurted out by a fellow who discovered the lighthouse on the chart, which kept disappearing from view, was marked as 110 feet above mean high water.) On the van ride back, we all agreed that the waves weren't really all that big: probably less than 5 feet or so. Now, as for the attack by that giant man-eating squid . . .

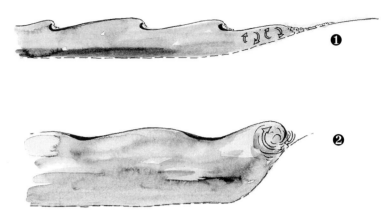

A gradual slope (**1**) allows the wave to spill gently as it nears shore. A sudden rise in slope (**2**) causes the wave to dump hard onto the shoreline.

the top layers are moving rapidly, waves may suddenly dump and hit the beach hard. Spilling waves are fun to surf and are fairly predictable; dumping waves are bad news.

Dumping waves are powerful: If you get caught during the crash, you can take a real pounding. I saw a kayak hull completely cave in and fracture in a dumping wave that was no more than 4 feet high. Even when paddling in deep water, keep an eye on the chart for sudden shallow areas such as ledges and reefs. These may create dumping waves when the wave energy is dissipated by an underwater obstruction.

Waves will also be affected as they hit and rebound off headlands and cliffs. A wave that rebounds from a steep headland may meet an incoming wave at just the right moment to create *clapotis*, a sudden slamming of two waves against each other. If you're in the middle, things can be very dicey. Headlands that are open to a long fetch are particularly dangerous, and they will create confused seas where wave energies meet and collide. Headlands may also spill wind from their heights, creating localized wind turbulence that can capsize an unsuspecting kayaker.

I had quite an education on these effects one fine paddling day. I sat outside the sloppy confusion and watched lines of wave energy approach, hit, and

rebounding waves

wave energy

headland

confused seas

Wave energies collide and rebound from obstructions such as headlands. This creates an area of turbulence and confusion.

rebound from a headland. At the same time I could see an offshore gust of wind spill from the land and "splash" onto the water, which further disturbed the confused surface. It didn't take much imagination to envision what would happen in stronger winds and bigger seas. Since headlands offer no refuge or safe landing,

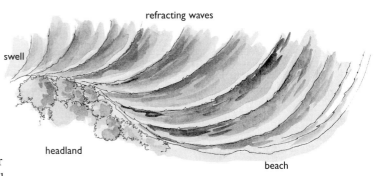

As waves encounter a point of land, they will bend, or refract, around this point.

you should have a healthy respect for these areas and stay well off their shores.

Waves not only rebound, but also bend, or refract, around points of land or islands. Think of a wave as a flow of fluid energy. Then predict where forces will be magnified and where they will be diminished. Choosing a landing site or picking your way along the coast could depend on how well you understand these forces.

Waves and tidal currents

I described what happens when one wave meets a rebounding wave. A similar reaction occurs when the wind meets an opposing tidal current. In this situation, wave height will increase and wave length will decrease. This creates steep waves that are a real hazard for sea kayakers.

This type of action commonly occurs at river mouths, especially during an ebbing tide. The strength and direction of the tidal flow, the depth of the water, and the wind's strength are factors. If you are pad-

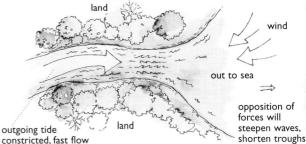

When a tidal current opposes the wind, waves will steepen and shorten. This is particularly noticeable at river mouths on a strong ebbing tide.

dling near a river mouth, especially a large river with a strong flow, plan to paddle at slack tide or in the early morning when the sun is not yet out and the wind is likely to be weaker. (See "Tides and tidal currents" starting on page 118 for more information.)

WIND

Weather reports state wind speed and direction. The wind's direction is given as a compass point (*e.g.*, north or southwest). This tells you where the wind is blowing *from*. The report also may describe the wind as an onshore wind or an offshore wind, which tells you where the wind is blowing *to*. Offshore winds are more challenging to sea kayakers than onshore winds. Facing a stiff headwind coming home can be discouraging. If you have any difficulties and no place to pull out, an offshore wind will push you farther from shore.

Beaufort wind scale

Beaufort number	Wind speed (knots)	Wind description	Water description	Land description
0	less than one knot	calm	flat calm	nothing stirring
1	1–3	light air	ripples	smoke drifts gently according to wind direction
2	4–6	light breeze	small wavelets	air movement can be felt on your face
3	7–10	gentle breeze	scattered whitecaps and large wavelets;	leaves and twigs in motion
4	11–16	moderate breeze	lots of whitecaps; small waves lengthen	loose paper blows around; small branches move
5	17–21	fresh breeze	mostly whitecaps with spray; moderate waves	flags ripple; small trees begin to sway
6	22–27	strong breeze	whitecaps everywhere; more spray	larger trees and branches move; whistling heard in sailboat rigging
7	28–33	near gale	foam from waves begins blowing in streaks; sea heaps up	whole tree sways; your skirt gets blown up around your face
8	34–40	gale	foam is blown in well-defined streaks; crests begin breaking	branches and twigs torn from trees; you have trouble making headway on foot
9	41–47	strong gale	dense streaking; spray reduces visibility	roof shingles peeled from houses
10	48–55	storm	sea begins to roll and look white; spray reduces visibility	trees uprooted; structural damage to buildings
11	56–63	violent storm	sea covered with white foam patches; large waves	widespread damage
12	64+	hurricane	air filled with foam and spray; almost no visibility	major, widespread damage

The wind's speed may be given in mph (miles per hour) or knots (nautical miles per hour). A nautical mile (6,076.12 feet) is greater than a statute or land mile (5,280 feet). Therefore, 1 knot is approximately equal to 1.15 miles per hour.

When you are given the wind speed, you should have some idea of what that wind velocity will do to water and how it will feel to you in your boat. The Beaufort scale was created in 1808 to indicate the effect wind would have on a full-rigged frigate under sail. Today, the Beaufort scale includes descriptions of the effect of wind on land features such as trees, a flag, etc. The wind is now defined by actual wind speed in addition to the original Beaufort system of "forces." These levels run from Force One to Force Twelve (see table, above).

The Beaufort scale outlines only what you can expect to see at different wind velocities.

It does not take into consideration fetch, swells, heavy rain, tidal current, and other factors. Being familiar with the Beaufort scale gives you a handy reference. Using that as a basis, you can then consider other factors that might enhance or diminish the wind.

Paddling in wind

Many of the same techniques I covered in "Staying on course" also apply to paddling in wind, since it is often the wind that sends you off course in the first place! Different wind directions will affect your boat in different ways. How wind affects your boat depends on your hull design and how it is loaded, so things are not always easily predicted. When you set out on a paddle, make sure your boat is loaded evenly and no objects have unusually high wind profiles on your deck (see "Packing your kayak," pages 140–142, for more on loading strategies).

Understanding the above-water and below-water forces on your boat will help you develop a strategy to control the boat in

DON'T LET IT GET YOU DOWN

While paddling in wind can be discouraging or distracting, the wind is *not* plotting to get you! It's not smart enough—wind is just air with an attitude. You can determine its direction, feel its force, and predict what changes you may see on the water. The more comfortable you become in wind, the less threatening it will seem. And if you're feeling unfriendly toward a particular bit of wind, head for home or declare a wind-bound holiday!

"**M**y most difficult time paddling in the wind was in the fall several years ago, paddling under the Golden Gate Bridge. It had been a terrific day, and we were paddling back to Sausalito. It felt like my boat had taken on a mind of its own—knowing I was tired after a full day of paddling with conditions becoming more significant. I found myself consciously making it a point to sit up more so I could use my torso effectively. But nothing seemed to work. We were paddling as a group and had gotten a bit scattered, so I sought guidance from my husband who was also in the paddling group. It was clear to me that my level of comfort was diminishing rapidly. I still remember the day clearly. I remember him helping with a minor rudder adjustment and assuring me that the entire group was finding it challenging as well. I sat up straighter than ever and concentrated on my forward stroke as I continued my path back to Sausalito with the group. The day and trip were fabulous. I learned more about paddling in very challenging wind and tidal situations than I had been exposed to before. And I learned I can do this. I'm hoping to return to 'Paddle the Gate' again soon."

—Deb Shapiro, co-owner of The Kayak Centre

wind. Forces created by headwinds may be obvious. But other forces, such as those created by crosswinds, are more complex. They may not seem intuitive at first.

Having a general strategy that you can use when paddling in different wind directions is useful, and it will save you frustration. You can't make the wind go away, but you can understand what is happening when you encounter it.

The first rule to remember when paddling in wind is to keep moving. You'll be less affected by the wind and better able to control your boat if you keep moving. Once you stop moving, you are at the full mercy of the wind, and it will be more difficult to restart. Try to maintain a steady cadence in your paddling and make your strokes shorter and quicker. Consider the wind's effect on your exposed paddle blade. You may want to keep your strokes lower in certain conditions. Remember where the power comes from in your forward stroke—this is not the time to "lily dip." Rotate your torso to drive your upper hand forward and use your legs to push on the footbraces for additional support and power.

Try to find places to hide behind if you need a breather from the wind. A small slice of land or a moored boat can be an effective windbreak. Be aware that a boat may swing on its mooring if you choose to hide there. When you leave the windbreak's protection, you need to make sure you have plenty of momentum as you reset your course. When you paddle in wind, you may need to make adjustments to your travel time and heading (see Chapter 8 for more on this topic).

Paddling into the wind

Paddling into the wind can be tiring. It can also be unsettling, because you can't afford to stop and lose your momentum. When you paddle into the wind, you may feel as if you are pushing against a solid wall and getting nowhere. Relax. The wind isn't a solid wall; there are holes you can find if you pay close attention.

Try to feel the rhythm of the wind and then work with that rhythm. The wind will have small gusts and moments of slack, even if the slack times last only for a second or two. Power your way through the moments of slack and maintain a steady cadence of strokes in the stronger gusts. You will make headway with this strategy. Look to the shore or to some other object off to the side to reward yourself. You'll see that you are indeed moving—even if you feel as if you're standing still. Visualize your paddling distance as a series of small steps. Mentally check off steps and reward yourself as you complete each one. Break into song to help set a steady rhythm.

Keep an eye out for windbreaks to duck behind for a quick breather. If you are paddling directly into the wind, you probably won't have too much trouble staying on course—just some difficulty maintaining your headway.

Paddling with the wind

It doesn't get any better than this! When you paddle with the wind at your back, everything seems quiet and surprisingly still. It isn't until you turn into the wind that you feel the wind's force.

Your main concern when paddling downwind is the presence of following seas. They can give you a free ride. But they can be unsettling, because your stern will suddenly lift and your boat may feel unstable. If you do experience following seas of any size, remember that—in all but the most severe conditions—you can control your position in the waves. If you are uncomfortable with the free but fast ride down the face of the wave, you can back paddle to let some of the wave pass underneath you. When you are in the trough of a wave, don't paddle hard to climb the wave's back face—you've got a free ride coming up! Maintain your position perpendicular to the waves and control your speed at a level that's comfortable for you.

You may find that your boat wants to turn to either side when your stern is lifted by a wave. You want to avoid turning parallel to the wave, or broaching. If you do broach on a wave, lean your boat into the wave by lifting the lower (or wave trough) side of your boat with your hips and knees and use your high brace to gain support on top of the wave until it passes. You will find it easy to turn your boat as a wave passes underneath you and you are at its crest. At that moment, your waterline is shortened and both ends of your boat are out of the water. Realign yourself and continue on your way.

Paddling in crosswinds

You will rarely be pushed directly sideways by a beam wind if you maintain forward momentum. You may, however, need to work harder to maintain your course in this type of wind. As you travel forward in crosswinds, you will notice that your boat will have a tendency to swing up into the wind, which can throw you off course. This is called weathercocking. (Leecocking, which is rare, occurs when the bow swings downwind. This may happen due to improper loading making the boat stern heavy.)

Weathercocking occurs in crosswinds as the bow reacts to a build-up of water pressure on its downwind side and swings to the lower pressure side, which is the upwind side. At that same time, your stern—which is freer to swing either way—is blown downwind. With these two factors acting in concert, your boat can have a definite tendency to swing up into the wind. Some boat designs need only a whiff of wind to begin weathercocking. Others hold their course more firmly.

Weathercocking can be frustrating, but there are strategies for dealing with it. Leaning your boat into the wind will help. Remember, when you lean your boat in

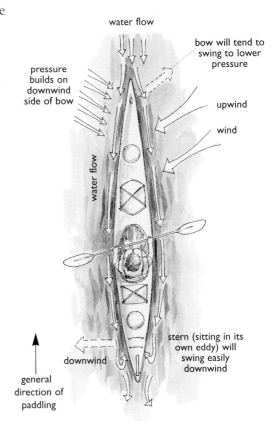

water flow

bow will tend to swing to lower pressure

pressure builds on downwind side of bow

upwind

wind

water flow

stern (sitting in its own eddy) will swing easily downwind

downwind

general direction of paddling

As a kayak moves through the water, it will tend to turn into the wind, or weathercock. The boat's design and the balance of weight aboard can affect this tendency.

one direction it will want to turn in the opposite direction. As you lean the boat into the wind, you can also lengthen your stroke on that side and make more of a forward sweep stroke. Make this stroke, however, within the normal range of your forward stroke. Keep the paddle low and be ready to brace if the waves build with this beam wind. Another way to combat weathercocking is to create more drag (or more area underwater) at the stern. This can be accomplished by dropping a rudder or skeg. While your boat may be slowed slightly, you will be able to maintain a more normal paddling cadence. If you are not yet comfortable leaning your boat, this may be your best, but more mechanical, strategy.

Keep the following things in mind when you are paddling in beam winds:

- Keep a steady cadence to your forward stroke and make your course adjustments early and often. This way, you will avoid losing momentum by having to make full turns.

- If you need a decisive course correction, make it at a time when you are being lifted by a wave and your waterline is shortened.

- In strong beam winds, the waves will be building and striking broadside. A boat lean into the wind will serve to stabilize your boat as the wave passes under you. If the wave begins breaking, you may have to resort to a high brace into the wave before continuing your forward stroke.

- Know how to control your boat without using a rudder (rudders break!). That said, it is also silly to not take advantage of a rudder when it really does you some good—such as when paddling in beam winds over a long crossing.

TIDES AND TIDAL CURRENTS

Sea kayakers need to become familiar with the terminology of tides and tidal currents in order to understand such resources as tide tables. Plus, you'll be able to "talk the talk" with local mariners, who are excellent sources for tidal information.

Here are the most common terms:

- **tide:** the vertical movement of water that is governed by the gravitational forces of the sun and the moon.

- **current:** the horizontal movement of water. If this movement is caused by the rise and fall of the tide it is called *tidal current*. (Outside of the United States the term *tidal stream* is used in place of *tidal current*. This avoids confusion with *ocean currents*, which are caused by thermal influences.)

- **ebb:** the fall of the tide. When the tide goes out it is said to be *ebbing*.

- **flood:** the rise of the tide. When the tide comes in it is said to be *flooding*.

- **slack:** the period during which the tidal current reverses itself and there is no discernible flow.

- **stand:** the point at which the tide goes no higher or lower. At the time of the stand, the water may continue to flow as it fills or drains areas beyond its location. Thus, a tide can be standing but not slack.

- **set:** the direction of tidal current flow. If the tidal current flows from west to east, the set is given as "easterly" or as a compass direction (090 degrees). (Note that this is exactly opposite from how wind directions are given; a wind blowing from west to east is considered a "westerly" wind.)

- **drift:** the speed of the tidal current, expressed in knots.

- **range**: the vertical distance between high and low water. Tidal ranges shift with the moon's position in relation to the sun and according to orbital variations of the earth and moon.

- **spring tide:** the maximum tidal range for a given area, which occurs when the sun and moon are in line. (This has nothing to do with spring as a season.)

- **neap tide:** the minimum tidal range for a given area, which occurs when the moon and sun are at right angles.

- **tide table:** a collection of data in tabular form that shows the height of the water at a particular location (such as a town) on a particular date. A tide table may also give corrections from a reference location so you can determine this information for nearby locations. A tide table can be as extensive as a large volume covering the east coast of North America or as limited as a brief table showing information for the local harbor and offered for free at your nearby marina.

- **tidal race:** an area where the velocity of the tidal flow is significantly increased by topographical features. These features may be entirely under water. A kayaker rarely wins a race with a tidal race.

Sea kayakers should understand and monitor tides closely. If you ignore them, you may find yourself trudging across mud flats to launch or slogging against a tidal current when you return home. Besides these inconveniences, currents created by the rise and fall of the tide can be dangerous and, when restricted, can produce fast-moving water that is far too swift for you to make headway against.

Tides also mean change. The appearance of islands and shorelines can be dramatically altered with the tides. At low tide, pieces of dry land can emerge to block your way. There's also a greater chance of rain developing during low tide, as a localized low-pressure area results from the receding water. While tides may originate in the open ocean where water masses are greatest, it is along the shoreline that you see their results.

Tides and tidal currents are forces to be reckoned with. As a sea kayaker, you will put your knowledge of them to work every time you go paddling.

Understanding tides and tidal currents

Because they can affect your speed and course, tides play a significant role in trip planning. When a tidal current runs directly opposite or directly in line with your boat's motion, it will have a maximum effect on your actual speed of travel (often called *speed made good*). When a tidal current is at a right angle to your boat's motion, it will have a maximum effect on your actual course of travel (*course made good*).

Many factors affect a tidal current's strength. The tidal current tends to be stronger where bays come together, since two bodies of water probably have different ranges and high-

Understanding tides and the timing of their rise and fall may be critical. Misjudging low tide might leave you slogging through mud and slippery rocks.

water times. Ebb tides usually are stronger and last longer than flood tides, because river flows feed an ebb tide but impede a flood tide. Tidal effects are magnified when water flows through a narrow channel or in areas where water flow is restricted. (When fluid is squeezed through a narrow area, it flows faster—just like your toothpaste coming out of the tube.) The middle time between hours for low and high tide shows the greatest movement and strength.

Obtain a tide table for the areas you plan to paddle in. This table will give you geographical reference points and the time and height of the water at particular points for each day of the year. Some include corrections for other points in between the reference points; this information used in conjunction with your chart will help you plan your outing. Local tide tables are easily obtained along the waterfront. More extensive volumes such as those published by International Marine are available from marine chandleries.

29

Eastport, Maine, 1998
Times and Heights of High and Low Waters

April

Day	Time	Height ft	Height cm		Day	Time	Height ft	Height cm
1 W	0137	21.7	661		16 Th	0118	18.8	573
	0806	-2.3	-70			0744	0.4	12
	1408	20.3	619			1344	17.9	546
	2030	-0.9	-27			2001	1.6	49
2 Th	0231	20.7	631		17 F	0200	18.6	567
	0902	-1.3	-40			0827	0.7	21
	1505	19.1	582			1428	17.6	536
	2126	0.2	6			2046	1.9	58
3 F ◐	0329	19.6	597		18 Sa	0246	18.3	558
	1000	-0.2	-6			0915	1.0	30
	1605	18.1	552			1517	17.4	530
	2226	1.2	37			2136	2.1	64
4 Sa	0431	18.6	567		19 Su	0337	18.1	552
	1101	1.0	30			1007	1.1	34
	1709	17.4	530			1611	17.3	527
	2329	1.9	58			2232	2.2	67
5 Su	0535	18.0	549		20 M	0434	18.1	552
	1204	1.2	37			1105	1.1	34
	1813	17.1	521			1710	17.6	536
						2332	1.8	55
6 M	0033	2.1	64		21 Tu	0536	18.4	561
	0639	17.7	539			1205	0.7	21
	1306	1.6	49			1810	18.2	555
	1915	17.3	527					
7 Tu	0133	1.9	58		22 W	0034	1.1	34
	0738	17.9	546			0637	19.0	579
	1402	1.1	34			1306	0.0	0
	2009	17.7	539			1910	19.2	585
8 W	0227	1.4	43		23 Th	0135	0.1	3
	0831	18.2	555			0737	19.6	604
	1452	0.8	24			1404	-0.9	-27
	2056	18.2	555			2007	20.3	619
9 Th	0314	0.9	27		24 F	0232	-1.2	-37
	0916	18.5	564			0834	20.7	631
	1535	0.5	15			1459	-1.7	-52
	2137	18.6	567			2100	21.4	652
10 F	0356	0.6	18		25 Sa	0327	-2.3	-70
	0957	18.8	573			0928	21.4	652
	1615	0.4	12			1552	-2.3	-70
	2215	19.0	579			2152	22.3	680
11 Sa ○	0436	0.1	3		26 Su ●	0421	-2.7	-82
	1036	19.0	579			1021	21.9	668
	1652	0.3	9			1643	-2.7	-82
	2251	19.2	585			2243	22.8	695
12 Su	0511	-0.1	-3		27 M	0514	-2.9	-88
	1112	19.0	579			1112	21.9	668
	1728	0.4	12			1734	-2.6	-79
	2327	19.3	588			2333	22.8	695
13 M	0548	-0.1	-3		28 Tu	0603	-3.5	-107
	1149	18.8	573			1203	21.5	655
	1804	0.6	18			1824	-2.1	-64
14 Tu	0003	19.2	585		29 W	0024	22.3	680
	0625	0.0	0			0654	-3.0	-91
	1226	18.6	567			1255	20.8	634
	1842	0.9	27			1916	-1.3	-40
15 W	0040	19.1	582		30 Th	0115	21.5	655
	0703	0.2	6			0746	-2.2	-67
	1304	18.3	558			1348	19.9	607
	1920	1.2	37			2009	-0.4	-12

May

Day	Time	Height ft	Height cm		Day	Time	Height ft	Height cm
1 F	0209	20.5	625		16 Sa	0135	19.1	582
	0840	-1.1	-34			0804	0.2	6
	1443	18.9	576			1405	18.1	552
	2104	0.6	18			2023	1.5	46
2 Sa	0305	19.4	591		17 Su	0221	18.9	576
	0935	-0.1	-3			0852	0.3	9
	1541	18.1	552			1454	18.1	552
	2201	1.5	46			2114	1.6	49
3 Su ◐	0404	18.4	561		18 M	0313	18.8	573
	1033	0.8	24			0944	0.4	12
	1641	17.5	533			1547	18.2	555
	2300	2.1	64			2209	1.5	46
4 M	0505	17.7	539		19 Tu	0410	18.7	570
	1131	1.4	43			1040	0.4	12
	1741	17.2	524			1645	18.5	564
						2308	1.2	37
5 Tu	0000	2.3	70		20 W	0510	18.8	573
	0606	17.4	530			1139	0.2	6
	1229	1.7	52			1744	19.0	579
	1839	17.3	527					
6 W	0059	2.2	67		21 Th	0010	0.6	18
	0703	17.4	530			0612	19.1	582
	1324	1.4	43			1239	-0.2	-6
	1932	17.6	536			1844	19.8	604
7 Th	0152	1.8	55		22 F	0111	-0.3	-9
	0756	17.6	536			0713	19.7	600
	1414	1.5	46			1338	-0.7	-21
	2020	18.1	552			1942	20.7	631
8 F	0240	1.3	40		23 Sa	0210	-1.3	-40
	0843	17.9	546			0812	20.2	616
	1459	1.2	37			1435	-1.3	-40
	2103	18.6	567			2037	21.6	658
9 Sa	0324	0.8	24		24 Su	0307	-2.2	-67
	0926	18.2	555			0908	20.8	634
	1541	1.0	30			1529	-1.7	-52
	2143	19.0	579			2134	22.2	677
10 Su	0404	0.3	9		25 M ●	0401	-2.9	-88
	1007	18.4	561			1001	21.1	643
	1620	0.9	27			1622	-1.9	-58
	2221	19.2	585			2222	22.5	686
11 M ○	0443	0.0	0		26 Tu	0453	-3.1	-94
	1045	18.5	564			1054	21.1	643
	1659	0.9	27			1714	-1.8	-55
	2258	19.4	591			2313	22.3	680
12 Tu	0521	-0.2	-6		27 W	0544	-3.0	-91
	1122	18.5	564			1145	20.8	634
	1737	0.9	27			1805	-1.3	-40
	2335	19.4	591					
13 W	0600	-0.1	-3		28 Th	0003	21.9	668
	1200	18.4	561			0635	-2.5	-76
	1815	1.1	34			1236	20.2	616
						1855	-0.7	-21
14 Th	0013	19.3	588		29 F	0054	21.1	643
	0639	-0.1	-3			0725	-1.8	-55
	1239	18.3	558			1327	19.5	594
	1855	1.3	40			1946	0.1	3
15 F	0052	19.2	585		30 Sa	0146	20.2	616
	0720	0.0	0			0816	-0.9	-27
	1320	18.2	555			1419	18.8	573
	1938	1.5	46			2038	0.9	27
					31 Su	0239	19.2	585
						0907	0.0	0
						1512	18.2	555
						2131	1.6	49

June

Day	Time	Height ft	Height cm		Day	Time	Height ft	Height cm
1 M ◐	0333	18.3	558		16 Tu	0253	19.5	594
	0959	0.9	27			0923	-0.4	-12
	1607	17.7	539			1526	19.1	582
	2226	2.1	64			2150	0.6	18
2 Tu	0429	17.6	536		17 W	0349	19.3	588
	1053	1.5	46			1018	-0.3	-9
	1702	17.4	530			1622	19.3	588
	2321	2.4	73			2248	0.4	12
3 W	0525	17.2	524		18 Th	0449	19.1	582
	1147	1.9	58			1115	-0.2	-6
	1756	17.4	530			1721	19.7	600
						2349	0.1	3
4 Th	0017	2.4	73		19 F	0550	19.1	582
	0621	17.0	518			1215	-0.2	-6
	1240	2.1	64			1821	20.1	613
	1849	17.6	536					
5 F	0110	2.1	64		20 Sa	0050	-0.4	-12
	0715	17.1	521			0652	19.2	585
	1331	2.0	61			1315	-0.4	-12
	1939	17.9	546			1920	20.6	628
6 Sa	0201	1.7	52		21 Su	0151	-1.1	-34
	0805	17.3	527			0752	19.5	594
	1419	1.8	55			1414	-0.6	-18
	2025	18.4	561			2017	21.2	646
7 Su	0248	1.1	34		22 M	0249	-1.7	-52
	0851	17.6	536			0850	19.8	604
	1504	1.6	49			1512	-0.9	-27
	2108	18.8	573			2112	21.5	655
8 M	0332	0.6	18		23 Tu	0344	-2.2	-67
	0935	17.9	546			0945	20.1	613
	1547	1.4	43			1604	-1.0	-30
	2149	19.1	582			2205	21.7	661
9 Tu	0414	0.2	6		24 W	0437	-2.4	-73
	1016	18.1	552			1037	20.1	613
	1629	1.2	37			1656	-0.9	-27
	2229	19.4	591			2255	21.6	658
10 W	0455	-0.1	-3		25 Th	0527	-2.3	-70
	1055	18.3	558			1127	20.0	610
	1709	1.1	34			1746	-0.7	-21
	2308	19.5	594			2344	21.2	646
11 Th	0535	-0.3	-9		26 F	0615	-1.9	-58
	1135	18.4	561			1216	19.6	597
	1750	1.0	30			1834	-0.2	-6
	2348	19.7	600					
12 F	0615	-0.5	-15		27 Sa	0033	20.6	628
	1216	18.5	564			0702	-1.3	-40
	1833	0.9	27			1303	19.2	585
						1922	0.3	9
13 Sa	0030	19.7	600		28 Su	0121	19.9	607
	0655	-0.6	-18			0749	-0.6	-18
	1259	18.7	570			1351	18.7	570
	1917	0.9	27			2010	0.9	27
14 Su	0114	19.7	600		29 M	0209	19.1	582
	0735	-0.6	-18			0836	0.1	3
	1344	18.8	573			1439	18.3	558
	2003	0.8	24			2058	1.5	46
15 M	0202	19.6	597		30 Tu	0259	18.3	558
	0816	-0.5	-15			0923	0.9	27
	1433	19.0	579			1529	17.9	546
	2055	0.7	21			2147	1.9	58

Time meridian 75° W. 0000 is midnight. 1200 is noon.
Heights are referred to mean lower low water which is the chart datum of soundings.

A tide table provides the predicted time and height of low and high tides in a given location.

Rather than challenge a tidal current, a smart sea kayaker either uses them in her favor or waits until slack tide, when there is little or no movement. Give special consideration to tidal currents that oppose the wind; in this situation the water becomes choppy and unruly. When both current and wind are strong, waves may steepen and shorten and be extremely dangerous to paddlers or small boats. When tidal currents run in the same direction as the wind, it can be equally challenging to paddle against their combined forces. Tidal current tables note the times of slack water and of maximum current (and its velocity in knots) at a series of reference points. You can also use the tables

A SIMPLE CALCULATION
• • • • • • • • • • • • • • • • • • •

To get an idea of the effects of tidal currents on your trip planning, consider this example:

Assume you paddle at a speed of 2.5 knots (nautical miles per hour). If you paddle directly *against* a 2-knot current, your actual speed (speed made good) will be a mere 0.5 knots. If you paddle *with* a 2-knot current, you will cruise at 4.5 knots. On this imaginary trip of 5 nautical miles, it would take you 10 hours if you traveled against the current; it would take a little over an hour if you had the current in your favor. With no current, it would take you 2 hours (5 miles ÷ 2.5 knots = 2 hours) to reach your destination.

While in practice the world is rarely this simple, these calculations do point out the significance of tidal currents. To ignore them amounts to poor planning.

to determine tidal currents for subordinate points. These resources are available for many areas from marine chandleries and paddlesports shops. If tidal current data is unavailable for your planned paddling area, question local paddlers or other boaters about tidal currents in the area and study your nautical charts and tide tables.

USING THE LAND: EDDIES IN THE OCEAN

Wasting energy when I'm paddling just doesn't make sense because it limits the distance I travel and the amount of time I can enjoy exploring on the water. Before I began sea kayaking, I had some experience in whitewater. I got used to hopping from eddy to eddy, ducking behind rocks, and shooting across currents at angles that required little more than a stroke or two at the stern. You can do the same thing on the ocean. The only difference is the areas are much bigger and their effects usually are not as pronounced.

An *eddy* is produced when there is an obstruction to the flow of water. Water flows around that obstruction, and a pocket is created behind the obstruction. Here, the water actually flows in the opposite direction as it attempts to fill this area. If you look behind a rock positioned in the middle of a fast-moving river or tidal race, you can see the water move back upstream. If the obstacle is a decent size, you can park your boat or several boats behind the rock and hang out. You will be protected from the current's flow with your bow gently bumping the backside of the rock.

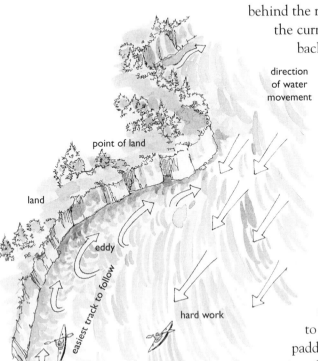

direction of water movement

point of land

land

eddy

easiest track to follow

hard work

Now imagine this on a grand scale: Instead of a rock, there is a long point of land; and instead of a river flowing downstream, there is a tidal current. You will have to expend less effort if you paddle in the area where the point of land protects you from the tidal flow. And if the flow is strong, you actually get a boost from the favorable current in the eddy.

As you paddle along the shore, look at the flow of the water. Is it helping you or working against you? Or is there no discernible movement? Not only is the area along the shore often a more interesting place to paddle but it can also be a less tiring place to paddle. Points of land and little nooks and crannies of shoreline will produce this eddy effect, and

Eddies created by a piece of shoreline can be helpful. Hugging the shoreline may be the longer, but easier, route when opposing a strong tidal current.

you might as well take advantage of them. These same land features may also serve as a wind-break.

You may be able to paddle more distance as you hug the shoreline and take advantage of these eddies. If the current has much push, you will probably make better headway than the person slogging ahead out in the channel. Conversely, if the current is in your favor, the best place to be is in the middle of the deep-water channel where the current flow is strongest. But other vessels use channels as their main "highways." If there is a lot of boat traffic, the channel is not an appropriate place for you to travel. (For more on shipping channels, see "Rules of the road and reality" pages 132–133.)

WEATHER

Most folks who spend a lot of time outdoors develop an extra sense about weather. They sniff the breeze knowingly and seem to sense the beginnings of electrostatic build-up long before a thunderhead is even visible. Developing this sensitivity takes years of experience and the willingness to systematically study cloud formations and light changes and relate them to both the weather forecasts and to what actually happens out there.

Weather is a fascinating study and a lifelong pursuit for the sea kayaker. If you haven't already, it is time to look skyward, sniff the breeze, and pay attention. You may not be able to forecast the weather, but you can understand and interpret weather forecasts and what you observe around you: a wind shift, cloud formations, dew on the morning grass. There are signs all around you that tell you about humidity levels, wind shifts, and changing barometric pressure. You just need to know where to look and then figure out what you saw.

Start gathering weather information regularly from television news (especially the radar and weather maps), radio broadcasts (particularly those by the National Weather Service), and Internet sites. You should also make a habit of observing the actual weather.

Consider keeping a weather observation diary, especially during paddling season. Note wind direction, speed, cloud patterns, barometric pressure, and specific weather phenomena. This long-term view will help you anticipate seasonal variations and the likelihood of certain patterns in your area.

Pay particularly close attention to weather forecasts several days prior to any paddling outing. Note any developing weather systems that might move into your region, and begin developing your own forecast for your trip dates.

Once you are at your launch site or on the water you may need to make quick decisions about the weather and your trip. Should you launch, continue, or change directions? As you paddle you will be monitoring a very small slice of the weather world—probably just a mile or two in any direction. No radio broadcast or weather map will pinpoint this area for you. A safe and successful trip will depend on your own observations and understanding of the weather.

Weather basics

My intent in this book is not to make you a weather expert. But it helps to understand some general trends regarding how weather works.

Weather patterns and their accompanying winds are created by the heating and cooling of the earth's surface. As surfaces heat and then cool, differences in atmospheric pressures occur across the given area. As air moves across this pressure gradient, always seeking equilibrium, wind is created.

On a local scale, a mainland shoreline may heat up during a sunny day. The air above the land heats and the warm air rises. The cooler, heavier air traveling across the water is pulled into this area and an onshore breeze, or sea breeze, is created. The same phenomenon may be reversed at day's end as the land quickly cools and draws in the now-warmer air from over the water. This process is a small example of what happens on a global scale. Equatorial air rises and begins its flow toward the earth's poles, and the cooler air from the poles flows underneath to replace it. This process is continuous. Coupled with the earth's rotation, this movement sets up weather patterns and their prevailing winds across the globe.

Differential pressures in the atmosphere will create ridges and troughs: areas of high barometric pressure and areas of low barometric pressure. These large "highs" and "lows" may measure several hundred miles across. High pressure areas bring fair weather and rotate in a clockwise direction. Low pressure areas bring unsettled or poor weather and rotate in a counterclockwise direction. You will see these areas marked on weather maps.

Besides being concerned with areas of low and high pressure, you must also consider air masses and the weather fronts created along the boundaries of two air masses of different temperature. Air masses collide and push each other around like two indefatigable bullies. As a front passes, there will be a change in the weather—usually a change for the worse. As a paddler, you should be aware of cold and warm fronts and their interactions. A front takes its name, cold or warm, from the dominant air mass behind it.

The movement of cold and warm fronts

The onset of a warm front is usually a drag, because a warm air mass will generally bring rain and unsettled weather for a period of time. But these fronts are slow to move into an area. Warm fronts are not usually associated with strong winds. You can expect the barometric pressure to drop steadily as a warm front approaches and then level off after the front's passage, gradually rising in its aftermath.

A cold front tends to move in like a freight train, and its edge can create localized squalls, hail storms, and high winds. The barometric pressure will begin to drop as the cold front nears. The intensity of the front is reflected in the severity of the drop. In the continental United States and lower Canada, you can expect the following: Just prior to the arrival of a cold front you should be able to detect a decided shift and strengthening in the wind toward the south and then southwest. After the cold front passes, the wind will continue to veer to the west and northwest.

Finally, it will come from the north. A wind is "veering" when it shifts in a clockwise direction. A wind is "backing" if it shifts in a counterclockwise direction.

After the passage of a cold front, temperature and humidity will drop dramatically and the barometric pressure will rise quickly. The air will clear to give you a beautiful but windy day. The passing of a cold front should always be cause for concern among paddlers because of the front's severity and suddenness. Pay attention to wind shifts and monitor the speed at which clouds move through the area. Keep an eye out for any ragged dark line of clouds, marking the front edge of a cold front. It holds nothing good for sea kayakers!

Clouds as messengers

Clouds can take on many forms—from grim to delightful. But they always serve as messengers for weather on the move. You need to learn to associate cloud shape, height, altitude, and color with particular weather patterns so you understand which clouds are sending you the signal to get off the water.

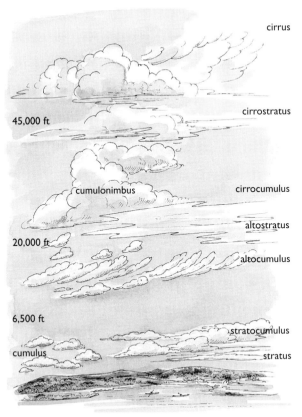

The shape, color, and altitude of clouds can tell you a lot about developing weather patterns.

The highest clouds, called cirrus clouds, may signal the first sign of turbulence aloft to portend a weather change a day or more away. If the cirrus clouds develop wispy "mare's tails," you know there is turbulence aloft. In general, as a wet weather pattern develops, clouds will thicken and be lower in altitude. Watch for these developments on the water, especially on multiday trips where you may need to alter your plans based on these signals.

A faster moving cold front will often overtake a warm air mass and force the warmer air swiftly upward as the cooler air wedges underneath. If the temperature difference of the two air masses is significant, this rising column of warm, moisture-laden air creates towering clouds that may be ragged along the bottom and appear to roll on the clouds' leading edge of nimbostratus clouds. The upper edge of the top cloud layer may seem to point with the wind's direction. When you see this, you are witnessing a cumulonimbus cloud formation with its telltale anvil shape that signals a thunderstorm. Get off the water immediately if it is moving your way. Thunderheads bring high winds and lightning, and their danger to sea kayakers is significant. Thunderstorms may also occur during summer months when warm, unstable air ascends the back of a stalled or departing cold air mass. Again, the dark clouds will tower ominously, with ragged edges along the bottom.

PAYING ATTENTION

· ·

We're going to take an imaginary sea kayak trip along the Maine coast for a long weekend. We'll move our camp each night and come back to our launch site on the third day. We have already packed all the necessary gear, plotted out our planned course for each day, and noted where we can pull out if things get nasty. Any areas open to camping are noted on our chart, as are the times of low and high water for each day.

More than a week before our trip, we began carefully monitoring weather reports—paying particular attention to any developing pattern for our intended path of travel. The reports were moderately promising. A warm front was expected to park off the coast several days prior to our launching and be followed with high pressure for the weekend. Translation: The warm front would probably bring rain and unsettled weather prior to our trip, maybe even stalling and staying during our trip dates. But the air temperatures would still be pleasant, so a little rain wasn't going to stop our trip. There is some concern about how strong the cold front that pushes through will be. The clear weather from the high pressure system following the cold front's passage will be welcome. But we don't look forward to any strong winds associated with it, so we'll keep listening to reports.

On the morning of our launch day, the air is still and hushed. The cloud cover is fairly solid but not low or threatening. As we load our boats we notice there is no early morning dew on the grass. We launch in negligible winds and paddle south toward our destination. With an ear to our weather radio we learn that the warm front appears to be parked just outside the area.

That evening around our cook fire we notice that the smoke from the fire hovers around the ground rather than rising in a column. The lack of dew on the morning grass tells us that the air is warm and moisture laden and rain is in the offing. The smoke curling down from our fire also predicts a storm on the way. The low pressure associated with rain is insufficient to suspend smoke particles and allow the smoke to rise straight upward.

That night, the cloud cover becomes thicker and lower and the wind shifts to the southeast. The winds are light, and they gradually shift to easterlies by midnight. Sometime during the night it begins to drizzle. The thickening, lower cloud cover tells us the clouds are laden with moisture and rain is near (in the summer). The wind coming from the southeast and then east suggests a counterclockwise movement of the system. Low pressure systems move counterclockwise and bring unsettled, wet weather.

The next morning it is raining so we are in no hurry to break camp and move on. We plan to paddle to our next destination—an island to the southwest of our present spot and farther from our launch site—by midday or so. Weather reports call for a gradual clearing by late evening with clear skies and light southwest winds expected tomorrow. By late afternoon the cloud cover begins to show holes with blue skies above, and the wind begins to come from the south.

But having an intended destination farther to the southwest is a cause for concern. The passage of the warm front and the wind now veering to the south suggests the cold front is on its way. If the cold front gains strength, the northwest winds we could expect on the backside of its passage might make it a tough slog back to the launch site the next day. We opt to move to our second choice: a site to our north and north of the launch site for our second night. We made our decision based on knowing there is a good chance the cold front is now moving rapidly into the area. The signs are all there: wind shift to the south, breakup of clouds and cloud movement. Knowing what to expect after the cold front moves through allows us to make a smart change of plans.

As we paddle north to our next campsite, the wind comes briskly out of the southwest, reinforcing our concerns about the cold front. Clouds have begun to break up and are moving rapidly. We keep our eyes peeled for any squall lines that might be heading our way. By the time we land and set up camp, the wind is

continued on next page

continued from page 126

gusting out of the southwest and a line of dark, ragged clouds is heading in our direction. The light seems to have changed, making things appear more pronounced and detailed, and everything is very quiet except for the gusting of the wind. Translation: The cold front is now roaring our way. Wildlife is quiet, humidity drops sharply, and the visibility is excellent just prior to the front passing through.

We make sure everything is battened down and covered as we watch the squall line move toward us. We discuss what to do if lightning is spotted. We'll all spread out, squatting close to the ground on our life vests, away from any tall trees or metal camping equipment. Boats are pulled up, turned over, and tied down. The squall line roars through with strong winds and pelting rain, but luckily no lightning. Within minutes the air clears and the temperature drops. The wind continues to veer to the west, blowing at an estimated 15 to 20 knots. These signs tell us that the cold front has now passed and the wind will continue to veer (move in the clockwise direction of a high pressure system) and may become gusty and strong. No more precipitation is expected, but the temperature will be considerably cooler.

The next morning the wind is gusting (we estimate around 20 knots with higher gusts) and strong, blowing out of the northwest. A few clouds skid across the sky. The sky is a beautiful blue and the air is cool and fresh. We load up and head back to our launch site, paddling close by the shoreline and its protection from the wind. We are very pleased with our choice to move our second campsite to the north. Paddling back to our

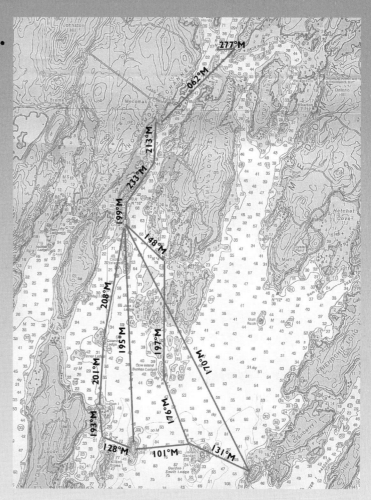

A good trip plan includes several contingency plans as well as a primary course.

launch site in the teeth of the strong offshore breeze would have been quite challenging. With the flooding tide it could have been downright nasty.

Paying attention to the forecasts, but more importantly to what we observed, has saved us a lot of grief. Paddling back in the short, steep waves that would result from the stiff offshore wind blowing against the flooding tide would have been tough. It even had the potential to be dangerous.

Fog

Whether you find fog eerie or soothing, you will still have to deal with it if you encounter it during your explorations.

Fog is simply a cloud close to the surface. It is made of water droplets that are suspended in the air and thick enough to obscure your visibility. There are two ways fog can be created: by warm, moist air passing over a cooler surface, or by cold air passing over a warmer, moist surface.

As a sea kayaker, you will be primarily concerned with only one type of fog: *advection fog*. Advection fog is formed when warm, moist air blows over cold water. As this air is cooled, water vapor condenses out of it and you have fog. This type of fog is often called coastal fog, because of its prevalence in areas where warm air from offshore waters passes over colder coastal waters. This type of fog is infamous. It has been described as "thick as pea soup" and "blue dungeon" fog, and it is the bane of many a boater. Advection fog does not "burn off." It requires a wind to send it on its way.

When people talk about fog burning off, they are usually referring to *radiation fog*, or ground fog. This type of fog occurs on cool, clear nights when the moist air close to the ground is cooled and spills into valleys and riverbeds. As it cools it condenses and creates low-lying fog. Often, a river or lake will continue to add moisture, increasing the likelihood of radiation fog in these areas. Radiation fog occurs only in calm air at night and is usually gone by midmorning, having lingered longest over bodies of water.

If you paddle in northern latitudes or in colder weather, especially on the edge of winter, you might encounter *sea smoke*. This type of fog is formed when very cold air flows over warmer water. The result is tendrils of vapor that are beautiful and, if the temperature difference is great, thick enough to reduce your visibility.

Paddling in fog

Besides reducing your visibility, fog can also distort sounds. A faraway motor may sound as if it is bearing down on you, while a nearby whistle may sound muffled. I have been spooked in the fog by what I thought was the sound of an approaching powerboat—only to sit for several minutes before realizing the boat was nowhere in my vicinity!

Your navigation skills must be sharp in the fog, and you must constantly take stock of where you are by referring to your chart and any nearby landmarks. Your bearings must be determined accurately, and your heading must be maintained or adjusted carefully (see "Navigation," Chapter 8). Consider hugging the shoreline if you can. You can also "buoy hop," or make your way from one buoy to another, to reach your destination. If might not be the most direct route but it offers the most checkpoints.

When paddling in the fog, it is critical that all group members stay together and have group whistle signals worked out in advance. You should also discuss what you would do if a member is lost. If someone is separated from the group, that person should hold still and signal the group, then listen for a return signal. The remaining members of the group should immediately raft up and be quiet and listen for the lost paddler's signals. Relive your summer camp days by setting up a buddy system before you get out on the water. It works.

THE SURF ZONE

If you are just starting out, the idea of entering the surf zone might sound as appealing as entering the Twilight Zone! But entering a surf zone can be great fun—assuming you meant to be there. We talked about how waves are created and how they build and either spill or dump as they near a sloping shore (see "Waves," page 110). Launching and landing through the zone where these waves break requires some water-reading skills and a definite plan.

Surf landings

If you are surfing for fun, you will want to catch a wave for a good ride and then turn around and head back out for another one. Paddling a loaded kayak on a multiday trip requires a more conservative strategy. If possible, sit outside the area where the waves are breaking and watch the waves that roll under you. Try to figure out the pattern of their size and timing by counting out seconds between each wave and noting whether the wave is smaller or larger than the previous one. You should be able to detect some pattern. Keep an eye to seaward, since larger waves break in deeper water.

I won't get into the mathematics of wave energy overlap and timing, but there is a greater probability that every seventh wave or so will be noticeably bigger. This is not the wave you want to use for your surf landing. In fact, you don't want to ride a wave in at all. You want to ride in on the back of the waves for a gentle landing.

As the wave passes under you, paddle on its backside while keeping a close eye over your shoulder to avoid getting picked up by the next wave. If you begin to pick up any speed down a wave face, simply back paddle until the wave passes under you. As you near shore, the water will get frothy and even a bit confusing. But by back paddling when you speed up and paddling forward after a wave has passed under you, you should be able to slowly pick your way into shore.

Once you have grounded on the shore, you

As you pick your way in through the surf, keep your boat perpendicular to the waves and be ready to back paddle to let waves pass under you.

GROUP SIGNALS

• • • • • • • • • • • • • • • •

When a group of paddlers is landing in surf, it is smart to use signals to coordinate the group. One paddler, usually one of the strongest, should land first. Once she has landed, she can use her upheld paddle to signal each paddler to come ahead. She can also provide directional signals needed for a safe landing. These signals should be agreed upon in advance. They can be useful for group communication any time you are on the water. Certain signals, shown here, have become standard.

Paddle signals are extremely useful on the water and during surf landings. These are several of the most common.

must move very quickly. Pop your sprayskirt and get out of the boat. Your kayak should be perpendicular to the shoreline. Then grab the bow toggle and pull the boat beyond the water's reach. Never get between your boat and the shore, in case your boat is picked up by a surging wave. If that happens, let go of your kayak and retrieve it after the wave has had its way with your boat. A kayak thrown toward shore is not something you should ever try to control or stop. Get out of its way and wait until it settles down.

Surf launchings

Before you try to launch into the surf zone, make sure you are ready. This is not the time to realize you put your paddle down just out of reach or that your life vest isn't zipped up! Be organized.

Set your boat perpendicular to the waves and pointed bow-out for launching. Position your boat so you get some water under it with each breaking wave but not enough water to throw you back to shore before you can get in the boat and seated. Get in quickly and attach your sprayskirt. Using your hands, keep hopping and pushing your way out until you have enough water to get some purchase with your paddle.

flat face of blade forward held aloft and still

paddle held aloft horizontal and still, with blade face(s) out

pointing to direction you should go (never toward problem or obstruction)

blade face held aloft, waved back and forth

Come Ahead/All Clear   Stop   Go This Way   Gaining Attention
                                                                                (problem, emergency)

Try to time your way through the waves so you do not find yourself at the spot where a wave is breaking. If your bow is lifted by a breaking wave, you could be thrown back to shore—rather spectacularly if the waves are big enough. Pushing through the surf zone is a time to be aggressive and keep your boat pointed straight out. As a wave breaks on you or in front of you, be ready to put your head down and put your paddle alongside your boat and close to the deck to "spear" through the wave. Don't ever hold the paddle over your head or in front of your chest. The force of a wave could shove your paddle back, and your paddle could slam you in the body or pull your shoulder out as you hold onto it. Always present the path of least resistance to a wave as you launch in the surf. When you come out the back side of the wave, paddle hard to clear this zone.

Surfing for fun

On the last day of a three-day school for novice paddlers, I watched as students' fears and anxieties were replaced with broad smiles after a few successful wave rides at a nearby beach. Surfing is a great confidence builder and a quick lesson in boat balance, braces, and the dynamics of waves and moving water. This section will not tell you about the intricacies of surfing. But I will give you some general guidelines on wave riding.

You should always wear a helmet (available from paddle-

Kayak surfing is a great way to polish skills and have fun. A sit-on-top design is a good choice because it's maneuverable and easy to use. (Courtesy of Ocean Kayak)

PLAYTIME

The first time I tried to surf, my husband and I chose to put in at a placid site about a mile from the beach where we planned to surf. As we neared the beach, my pulse rate increased with the noise of breaking waves. I began to wonder why I had thought this would be so much fun.

I sat outside the surf and watched it break on shore. It was thrilling to watch, but I wasn't ready to be a part of it. Thinking about surfing had been a lot more fun than being faced with the real thing. After some cajoling by Vaughan, I paddled a little closer to the beach so my boat was lifted and dropped as each wave passed. I sat there but couldn't bring myself to catch that first wave.

Then I saw several kids run out from the beach and body surf their way back to shore, laughing and screaming in excitement. And there I sat in my drysuit, sprayskirt, and helmet! I felt silly. After all, this was just playtime. I caught the next wave and picked up speed down its face toward the beach. I screamed. I laughed and hooted. I surfed until my arms felt like noodles and I was crusty with salt. Sure, I got tossed around a bit; I swallowed some water and got some up my nose. But so did the other kids!

USING THE RULES WITH COMMON SENSE

• • • • • • • • • • • • • • • •

Since kayakers were rarely considered when the rules of the road were written, we often fall outside their intended use. You sometimes need to use your own common sense when interpreting the rules and how they apply to kayaks.

I once was the co-leader of a kayak trip with someone who had taken several courses on navigation and U.S. Coast Guard regulations. This person, who was from the same area as I, insisted on trying to lead our group across and down a busy channel between the buoys—as if we were supertankers. Powerboats and sailboats were buzzing around us, and the group was being pounded by boat wakes and their rebound from a nearby breakwater.

I questioned his wisdom, politely at first. But I was told that "Everyone knows about red, right, returning" before he muttered something about where was I from (or maybe it was where I could go). I gathered the group as best I could and explained that they could follow his foolish course, or they could use their own brains and remain outside the channel (God forbid, to the left of the green can buoys!) and

continued on page 133

sports shops) and choose your surf spots carefully. The wave breaks should be consistent, and the surf should send you onto a soft shoreline. If the waves look too big or threatening, wait them out. A change in tide may flatten them a bit. By the same token, be aware of steepening waves that may begin to dump with the changing tide and be ready to call it a day.

One way of approaching surfing is to use a sit-on-top kayak. Many of these models are surfing machines and are easy to maneuver in waves. Adding thigh straps will give you better lower body control over the boat's motion and allow you to carve turns as the kayak speeds along the wave face. Using your brand-new composite sea kayak for surfing isn't the best choice. Shorter, nimble boats are more fun and less likely to be damaged if things get a bit rough.

RULES OF THE ROAD AND REALITY

I often hear kayakers sneer at large powerboats, claiming that because their kayak is human-powered they have the right of way. They may well have the right of way—but it will have to be their estate that brings that claim to court for them. Travel on inland and coastal waters is covered by maritime rules of the road. Think of it as a combination of traffic laws and etiquette.

Most regulations in place rarely acknowledge the existence of kayakers, and many boat skippers are not used to seeing these small craft plying the waters. You should use some common sense and courtesy when protecting your rights on the water. Kayakers are more maneuverable, and we have the least draft of any vessel on the water. We can therefore pull aside to let other vessels pass and hold our crossings until all is clear. Other boats with more speed or those that rely on the wind for their power will appreciate your thoughtfulness. Working vessels such as lobster boats, draggers, and shrimp boats should always be given the right of way when they are working.

Many larger harbors and ports have shipping channels, which are marked both on the charts and on the water by a system of buoys. Kayakers rarely belong in these channels, except for swift crossings when all is clear. If you must paddle in one of these shipping channels, stay well over to the edge noted on the chart for travel in your direction and keep a

Large boats stay in deep-water channels, often marked by buoys shown on your chart. Kayakers should stay outside these channels and away from their heavy traffic.

sharp lookout at all times (especially astern). In general, stay to the sides of channels or outside them when entering or exiting any harbor.

The saying "red, right, returning" might be engraved into your brain from a past navigation course. This means you should keep the red nun buoys on your right when returning to a harbor since these buoys mark the right-hand edge of the channel. That saying applies to boats large enough to require the deep water of a channel. Kayakers should paddle only at the far right edge of the channel and consider paddling outside of the right-hand edge if there are no hazards there. To find out about hazards such as rocks, shoals, underwater obstructions, and so on, you can consult your chart.

continued from page 132

enjoy their paddle into this busy, picturesque harbor.

Most of us who took the latter option had fun and even stopped to watch an osprey hover and dive at its prey. The others, following rules but not common sense, were completely frazzled by the large boats that surrounded them as they made their way down the channel.

This story is not told to incite insurrection and disregard for the regulations. But a more prudent course of action may be available to you as a kayaker.

Chapter 8

HIT THE WATER TRAIL

For many, the allure of sea kayaking is the ability to take off for parts unknown and explore. Oceans, islands, and shoreline provide a vast territory for exploration, and the sea kayak is a marvelous choice for minimizing the impact of that exploration. Seaworthy and nimble, it is a craft that leaves little or no imprint on the areas it touches.

Traveling by sea kayak requires some intelligence. There has always been a standing joke between sea kayakers and whitewater kayakers regarding respective IQs. Sea kayakers point out that whitewater boaters need only remember what color car they drove to the site that morning to find their way home. For sea kayakers—well, it is a little more demanding . . .

NAVIGATION

Theoretically, navigation is a simple procedure for sea kayakers. We review a nautical chart of our paddling area, plot a course that will give us something to point at, and use our deck compass to keep from going astray. These procedures work in a straightforward manner a great deal of the time. But the effects of wind, current, and fog—and the challenge of matching a bird's-eye chart view to an actual on-the-water view—can make the process trickier. You can estimate the effect these factors will have on your progress and make adjustments to your course. You can do some of this advance and some while under way. You will get better at the process with more paddling time under your belt. It is a fun and satisfying mental exercise.

This book is not an instruction manual on navigation. There is already an excellent book available: David Burch's *Fundamentals of Kayak Navigation* (The Globe Pequot Press, 1993). Burch's work is detailed and useful and goes well beyond the fundamentals. The mechanics of navigation are quite simple, however, and I will cover here the general process for finding your way on the water.

Using nautical charts

Unless you are paddling in a very small body of water, you will want to review a nautical chart of your paddling area. Nautical charts are maps of the ocean and its shores and are available at most paddlesports shops and marinas. These charts are packed with valuable information. As you gain more experience and understand more what to look for, you will be able to pull more and more information from a chart.

Charts include a system of symbols and abbreviations that tell you about landmarks, buoys, the nature of the ground beneath the water, the depth of water, and more. Chart No. 1 is not a chart at all; it is an explanation of the symbols and abbreviations used on charts. Published by NOAA, it is available where charts are sold. Chart No. 1 is something every sea kayaker should have in her library.

When you look at a chart, note any restricted passages where the current might be racing, headlands that might spill wind or (if exposed to a long fetch) create confused seas. Check the contours and descriptions of the shoreline exposed at low tide. Are these areas mud, sand, exposed rocks, or a steep wall with no obvious bailout possible? What would you expect to see at high tide? Are there any river mouths that must be navigated?

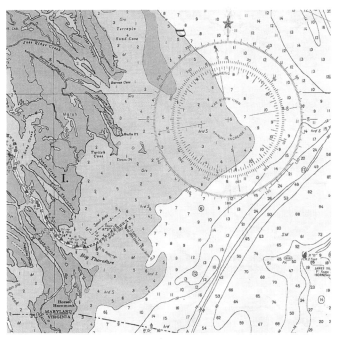

A nautical chart provides a wealth of information about an area and can show you where you are as you paddle and explore.

Imagine you are sitting in your boat in the area you plan to paddle. Are there geographical features along the way—such as a steep hill or a solitary island with a recognizable shape—that you can use as reference points? Look at the contour lines and shapes of the land features along your route and visualize how they will appear from your cockpit. On a chart, landmarks and land masses look clear and distinctive. From a kayak cockpit, these details of land are piled one upon

Relating what your chart shows to what you actually see from your kayak takes practice and experience. (Courtesy International Marine)

the other and may melt together into one giant shoreline! With experience, you learn to translate a bird's-eye chart view into your on-the-water view.

Note the navigational aids along your way: buoys, day beacons, lighthouses, sound signals on buoys, and other chart markings of use. It is hard to be lost when you paddle by a buoy. The chart gives you the specific shape, color, and number of each navigational buoy; thus, you will be able to pinpoint your position when you are near a navigational buoy. The order in which you encounter these buoys or markers can also be a significant clue. The buoy numbers increase as you move from the seaward side into a more restricted area. In poor visibility, you can use buoys as checkoff points along the way by plotting a course from one to the next.

Charts are published with different scales that determine how much of a given area is included on a single page. As on any chart or map, the scale is simply a ratio of units of measurement. The units themselves don't really matter—it's the ratio comparison that's important. Since sea kayakers don't cover many miles in a day of paddling, charts with a scale of 1:40,000 work well; this ratio gives plenty of detail but covers enough area so you'll typically stay on one chart over a few days of

Buoys and other navigational markers are invaluable when pinpointing your location. Their color, shape, number, and light or sound signals are noted on your chart. (Courtesy Bill Brogdon)

paddling. In this scale, 1 "unit" on the chart equals 40,000 "units" on the water. Most people choose to work with a unit of measurement that's easy to envision; for instance, 1 inch on the chart equals 40,000 inches on the water (or a little over 0.5 nautical miles).

You can also use the latitude scale on the edge of the chart to determine distances. For our purposes, one minute of latitude is equal to one nautical mile. (In actuality, a geographical mile of 6,087.2 feet is defined by one minute of latitude at the equator and is a tad longer than our nautical mile, pegged by international standards to be 6,076.12 feet. But it's close enough for our purposes.)

Before setting out, you must know how long it should take you to arrive at a given spot and thus what distance is reasonable to paddle in a day. Most sea kayakers are safe to estimate their touring speed at around 2.5 knots (which means you travel 2.5 nautical miles in one hour). This is a very easy pace that allows for sightseeing. To arrive at your own cruising speed for greater accuracy, determine a point-to-point nautical mile on a chart and then time yourself as you travel the mile-long distance.

The compass rose

When you look at a chart you'll notice several large (usually purple) circles that look like compasses. These devices, called compass roses, are made up of concentric circles, each of which is divided into 360 degrees. The outer circle, or true compass rose, includes a star pointing to true north. The middle

circle, or the magnetic compass rose, aligns with magnetic north and is the one you will deal with as a sea kayaker.

This all has to do with the difference between true north (the direction of the geographical North Pole) and magnetic north (where your compass needle points, slightly off to the side of magnetic north). The difference between the two is constantly changing; this difference is referred to as *variation*. As sea kayakers we operate in a relatively small area and can use a compass and a chart's magnetic compass rose without worrying about converting between true and magnetic compass points. Larger vessels or boats traveling over long distances, on the other hand, must consider the variation when plotting a course.

You'll learn more about all this as you continue your education in navigation. But remember this: If you ever need to relay your heading (the direction your vessel is pointing) or bearing (the direction from your vessel to some object), state the numbers distinctly and then say "magnetic." This way, everyone will be speaking the same language.

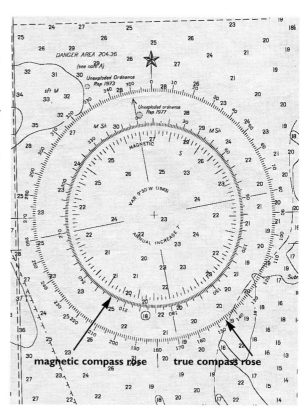

Use the middle circle of a compass rose on your chart to determine your bearings. The numbers there are noted as *magnetic* and will correspond to what you read on your compass as you paddle to a destination.

Tools for navigating

In addition to your chart and compass, there are several tools that come in handy when planning a trip and plotting your course. Some tools are great for planning at the kitchen table; others are useful when you're under way, working from your cockpit. Many high-tech tools, such as Global Positioning System (GPS) units are touted as being able to replace the charts and compasses of old—but your chart and compass will never run out of battery power. What's more, navigating using these simple tools is satisfying in a way that punching a button and viewing a lighted screen will never approach.

- **chart case:** a waterproof envelope with a clear window on at least one side. You can slide your chart inside and clip the case to your forward deck rigging or stash it below. Keep it where it's always easy to refer to at a glance.

- **parallel rules:** a set of two rulers (usually clear) held a distance apart, but parallel, with hinges. Parallel rules help you determine the bearing between two points. Holding one ruler steady against the chart at your starting point, you can slide the other forward as far as the hinge allows; then hold that one steady and slide the other forward. Repeat the process (called "walking") to the nearest compass rose and place the edge of the forward ruler through the center of the rose. Imagine a line along that ruler edge running through the center to a point on the compass rose; that point, shown in degrees, is your bearing. (Remember: Middle ring shows magnetic course, outer ring shows true course.)

  Parallel rules are great at a desk or table but unwieldy on your kayak deck. Acetate sheets with a series of parallel lines etched on them, often called "coursers," work great when under way. You can make your own or buy them from a marine supply shop.

- **dividers**: a device consisting of two sharp points hinged together at one end. Dividers allow you to lock in a unit of measure and walk it around your chart. You simply place one end at point A and the other at point B and use the chart scale or latitude scale to calculate the distance. You can also set the dividers to a specific distance using the chart scale and then walk the dividers along your course to determine its length. Use a small increment to make it easier to round islands and follow your actual course on the chart.

  Here's a neat trick that's handy when under way: Mark a piece of string with distance increments and attach it to your chart case. Instead of pulling out your dividers, you can run the string along your course to determine distances between points. This allows you to follow the dips and twists that are typical of

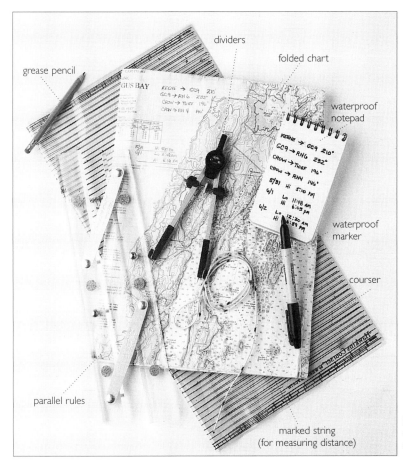

Here are some of the tools for developing your trip plan and plotting your course.

a day of paddling. If you change charts, make sure you check the scale and change your string if necessary.

- **grease pencil:** a waxy pencil. These are great for scribbling bearings and other notes on a chart case or even on your deck. The marks won't be washed away by splashes, but you can rub them off with a cloth or your finger.

Using a range

When you are under way, you can line up two stationary objects that are some distance in front of you and along your line of travel. This is called creating a *range*.

For example, let's say there are a steeple and a smokestack on land along your line of travel, one behind the other. If you are paddling straight toward them, you can use them as a range. As long as the two are aligned, you are on course; if they no longer appear aligned, you know you have drifted off course.

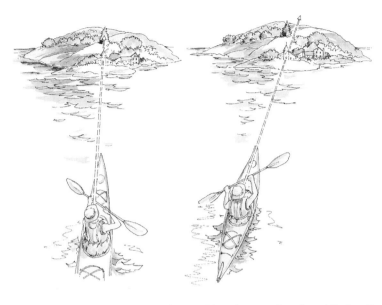

You may create a range by aligning two objects along your line of travel. You're off course if they're no longer aligned. Here, the boat must move to the right to get back on course.

If the farthest object in your range drifts to the right of the closer object, you are to the right of your course. Move your boat to the left until the objects realign. If the farthest object appears to the left of the nearest object, move right to bring them back in line.

Occasionally, ranges are noted on a chart as navigational aids. These ranges usually mark safe passages for larger vessels that have restricted movement. Using these ranges may keep a vessel in a deep channel or on a safe course around a bend in a heavily traveled river. Other objects such as spires, smokestacks, and buoys can also provide ranges on a chart; simply extend a line through two such objects into your paddling area to create a line of position. If these objects appear aligned as you are paddling, you are someplace on that line.

You may also create a range while under way to help monitor your course. When you do so, a small amount of drift to one side or the other is easily noted. Looking ahead to a single object won't give you nearly as much feedback about the need for course corrections.

PACKING YOUR KAYAK

How you load your kayak may determine how it performs on the water—and it will certainly determine how annoyed you get when it is time to find something. In terms of organizing your gear, you should consider some type of system so you can tell what is in each drybag without having to look inside each one. You may not need to know which particular shirt is in which bag, but you do need to know if a particular bag holds clothing or your first aid kit. Some paddlers color code their drybags or place a label made of duct tape on the exterior.

Before leaving home, repackage your food to minimize the amount of trash you'll generate on your trip. Avoid buying wasteful packaging when you shop, and repackage food in zip-top bags or containers prior to your trip. Remember to include any directions or dietary information you might need. Organizing food is where most people new to wilderness camping go wrong. Use small containers to organize the items you'll need every day and group each day's food together for easy access. If you can't find the peanut butter on your third day out without unpacking the entire boat, you need to review your method of organization.

What you carry on deck must not block your access to safety gear or prevent you from doing a solo or assisted reentry. Nothing on your deck should have a high profile to the wind or drag in the water. Heavy items do not belong on deck where they will raise your boat's center of gravity and, in rough water, make you regret their presence.

Before you pack, separate items into heavy items, non-compressible items, and things you expect to access during the day. Heavy items (such as jugs of drinking water) should be carried low and close to the center of the boat and should be held firmly in place by other gear. As you load your boat, keep in mind that the weight must be evenly distributed from side to side and fore to aft. Look at your boat in the water to make sure it is properly trimmed. If not, shift things around. You have to get this right before setting out for the day, because you can't correct it easily when you're on the water. Lean the boat to either side and make sure nothing shifts suddenly. A large container of water that shifts suddenly to the side may send you over or make your Eskimo roll a halfway proposition.

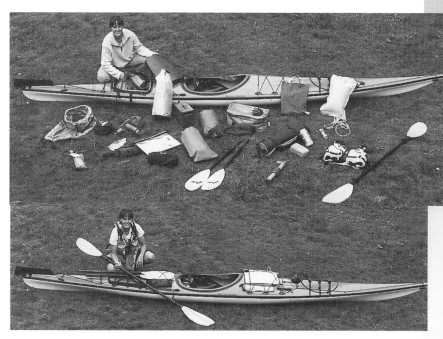

You'll be amazed at the amount of gear you can fit inside your kayak. But you must carefully balance the load and keep safety gear accessible.

PLAYING THE "WHAT IF" GAME

Anytime you go paddling, you should have a float plan. Your float plan may be as informal as telling your roommate that you are going out for a two-hour paddle in the harbor. For a multiday trip, your float plan might be formalized and show expected stopovers and a plotted course for each day of travel. Either way, someone on shore should be aware of your plans.

It is easy to do your planning at the kitchen table, plotting a course on your chart and noting your bearings from intermediate points along the way. Doing this type of planning as the fog envelops you or as a squall line approaches is not easy. Do you really want to be out there making decisions under challenging conditions that are demanding your full attention? Not me!

Before I leave home, I play the "what if" game. I review the chart and wonder what I will do if the wind kicks up from a given direction or if a thick fog settles in. Then I note the bearings to and from a variety of objects that will be there for me if things do go awry. I mark bailout points for different wind directions, and I mark intermediate stops in case the wind is wearing me down. It is a lot

continued on page 142

continued from page 141

easier to solve these problems at my kitchen table than it is to find solutions out on the water. In case of fog, I will have bearings over small distances to unmistakable objects like buoys. That way, if I get disoriented, it will be short lived. It is difficult to plot a course from your kayak. About all you can do is point your nose at something, note the compass reading, and then paddle that compass heading. But in fog, you may not have anything to point at and doing accurate chart work on your deck is not easy.

Use a grease pencil to record all your notes and bearings on your chart case or pencil them on an index card that you put inside the case. Rather than carry a full chart, consider cutting a chart into manageable pieces and then laminating them. You can also buy waterproof charts. Remember to include a section of the latitude scale on the side of the chart to help with your distance determinations and note the scale of the chart as well. Your chart section should also include a compass rose for quick reference and to help you determine a bearing while under way.

Playing the "what if" game can buy you valuable time on the water and allow you to relax. If difficulties arise, you already have a plan for how to deal with them.

In general, a good strategy is to pack things in small amounts. Instead of a 5-gallon water jug, pack two 2.5-gallon jugs. Or, better yet, pack five 1-gallon containers for more packing options. Carry a large mesh bag or duffel that you can use to transport all the small pieces to and from a landing or launch site. This saves trips to and from your boat and allows you to organize what you bring to the campsite. Whenever possible, use compressible containers such as drybags, soft coolers, and water bladders rather than rigid cases and jugs. Your packing options will be greater.

Make sure anything you carry in your cockpit is tethered or secured to the boat in some way. Velcro works well for small items such as flare packs and flashlights. You can use bungee strapping forward of your feet to secure things such as your tent. No matter how watertight your hatches are, I would always use drybags for those items that can't get wet: camera, sleeping bag, clothes, and so on.

Use the natural refrigeration of your boat to keep things fresh by putting perishables in the coolest spots along the keel line and insulate them with other gear. Freeze entrees at home and then pack them with later meals on the bottom. Use old pieces of foam padding to insulate water bottles and other containers as needed.

A WORD ABOUT WATER TRAILS

In the past decade, water trails have been developed throughout North America. There are water trails along Maine, Washington, Lake Superior, the Hudson River, Chesapeake Bay, Monterey Bay, and more. These trails are of great benefit to sea kayakers. They protect not only the waterways that we paddle, but the land alongside and our access to it.

Water trails often are a combination of public and private lands opened under certain restrictions (usually, membership in a water trail association). Campsites and other landing sites are spaced along the trails. Sea kayakers have embraced water trails and comprise the largest constituency in many water trail organizations.

Water trails are varied: There are short snippets for urban

paddling and exposed stretches of bold coast in remote areas. Rarely are water trails fully funded by a government agency. They are almost always maintained and monitored by the people who love them and use them. These volunteers give untold hours to serve as stewards for these waterways and their campsites, and all small boaters benefit.

You won't find water trails marked on your chart. But if you sign up as a member of a water trail organization, your membership most likely will include detailed information on campsites, launching areas, route selection, and protected species along the trail. In return, you will

"**V**ery few people will actually travel an entire water trail, but the very fact of a trail's existence is a siren for at least a few days' travel. Maine was extremely lucky to have the island resources around which to create a trail. Others may be less fortunate—they may have to think more creatively about what constitutes a trail, especially in more populated areas."

—Tamsin Venn, kayaking author and publisher of *Atlantic Coastal Kayaker*

serve as a steward for trail sites and be asked to volunteer for a variety of tasks. You will also be expected to abide by the organization's low-impact use policies, which address waste disposal, fires, length of stay, and other concerns.

Find out from paddlesports shops or other boaters if there is a water trail in your area. If there is, please consider donating your time and skill to protect it. If there isn't a water trail in your area, consider creating one. The process is demanding and doesn't happen overnight. But if there is enough interest and dedication, it will happen. See the Resources section, page 153, for more on water trails.

One of the reasons water trails thrive, even in this age of "No Trespassing" signs and liability concerns, is that people who use the trails are taking good care of them. Many areas designated for a water trail are showing improvement, even with increased use, because that use is thoughtful and low impact. Instead of toilet paper and charred tinfoil, there is now a logbook where someone describes the joys of watching seals cavort on a half-tide ledge.

A LOW-IMPACT VESSEL

Paddlers should be as low impact as their craft. Sea kayaks leave no oil sheen or noise in their wake. Paddlers should also leave no trace of their passing by adhering to low-impact techniques, which take the land, water, and wildlife into account for every action and minimize the impact of humans whenever possible.

Give wildlife a wide berth—especially mothers and their young, who are at their most fragile. Nesting sea birds are susceptible to sea kayakers who may unknowingly approach a shore and scare mothers from the nest. Nearby predators then have the opportunity to wreak havoc and destroy what may have been a fragile species' breeding potential for an entire season. If disturbed, marine mammals waste valuable energy, and the young may become separated from their parents and be at risk.

While I was working on this book, a friend called to tell me a heartbreaking story. He and his girlfriend were paddling and came across a mother eider and her young. They unknowingly got too close, and the mother eider dove under the water. The babies tried to dive, but they were too buoyant and nearby gulls attacked the young and carried them off before the mother had even resurfaced. My friends were devastated to think they had caused the chicks' deaths. Sometimes, heightened awareness comes at a high price.

One of the rewards of kayaking is the ability to observe wildlife. But we need to be aware that we have the potential to do harm. If the wildlife detect your presence and react to you, you are probably too close. Get a good pair of binoculars and enjoy observing their natural behavior— not their reaction to humans. If you must pass close by any wildlife, do so quietly and use low angle strokes, or coast if possible to minimize the disturbance you make. Be aware of any governmental regulations protecting particular species and abide by these at all times.

We also need to be careful of our impact on any fragile soils in wilderness settings. For example, the soil on many islands along the northeastern coast of the United States is thin and unable to withstand much traffic without showing signs of compaction and loss of vegetation. This thin soil is also incapable of breaking down human wastes, so campers must pack out their own waste when traveling in some of these areas.

Before setting out on any trip, make sure you know:

- the practices recommended for waste disposal;

- whether campfires are appropriate;

- whether any protected species reside in the area;

- what restrictions apply to tent site location and group size.

These considerations should always be a part of your trip planning. Others following in your wake will be glad you made the effort.

Chapter 9

TIPS AND MORE TIPS

As I developed this book, I kept setting certain subjects aside. It was not that they lacked importance: They just never fit in anywhere obvious. I couldn't bear to ignore these tidbits that have made paddling easier for me and others, and I would not leave out subjects of particular importance to women. You may be looking for some good stretches to add to your paddling workout. Or you might be wondering how you're going to pee within the confines of your cockpit or drysuit when faced with a long crossing. By now, you've gotten comfortable in your boat and have some paddling under your belt, and you have time to look at the little details. Well, here they are!

STRETCHES FOR PADDLERS

If you have any background in athletic endeavors, you know the value of stretching. As a kayaker, you should stretch before and after you paddle. Before you stretch, get your muscles warm by doing a few quick jumping jacks, waving your arms around, running in place, or "air paddling." Once they are warm, your muscles will stretch more easily, and there is less chance of a muscle strain.

Before getting in your boat, grab your paddle and try the following stretches.

Hamstrings

The backs of your legs will often get tight as you sit in your boat for long periods of time. To stretch, sit on the ground in your diamond-shaped paddling position. Lean slowly forward and reach out with your paddle toward your ankles. Hold this stretched position for at least 20 seconds and then gradually ease off. Do this several times, always taking care to use slow and controlled movements throughout the exercise. You can also do any number of hamstring stretches you might know from running or other sports to augment your paddling hamstring stretches.

Hugging your boat is a good lower-back and hamstring stretch. Your boat will appreciate it, too!

Torso

Since so many strokes and maneuvers rely on your torso rotation, you need to remain loose throughout your torso and hips. Use the same seated paddling position you use in your boat to sit on the ground. Swing your torso, with the paddle squared to your shoulders, around to the side of your imaginary boat. Hold this position for at least 20 seconds and then move to the other side for the same stretch. Do at least three of these stretches on each side.

Use your paddle as leverage against the side of your boat to stretch your lower back and torso.

Next, swing your paddle and torso over to one side. Using your forward-most blade, touch the ground alongside your foot. Use the blade against your foot and press outward with your upper hand to stretch your torso and lower back. Hold this position for 20 seconds. Then do the same on the other side. This is my favorite stretch; I also use it when I am in my boat.

Another good torso stretch requires the use of a paddling partner. Get in a standing back-to-back position with your paddling partner. Both of you then twist your torsos and reach around the side until you can touch palms, like playing "patty-cake." Do this on both sides several times.

You may feel silly doing this at a public launch site, but it's okay—other boaters think kayakers are strange anyway since we don't have motors on our boats!

Lower back

Stand with your feet about shoulder width apart and your knees slightly bent. Lean forward and let your arms and head dangle down toward the ground. (This will also stretch your hamstrings.) Hold this for at least 20 seconds. Begin to straighten very slowly and try to imagine each vertebrae dropping into place, starting from your lumbar region and working up to your neck. Do this very slowly over a full minute and continue to let your arms and head dangle until you are fully upright. Then lift your head.

You can do another lower back stretch in your boat's cockpit by leaning slowly back and, if possible, resting your upper body on the back deck. Relax on the back deck for a while and then sit up slowly. It helps to keep your eyes open so you don't get vertigo and capsize!

Wrists

You can do this stretch anywhere. Use one hand to pull your fingers back toward your forearm and hold them for at least 20 seconds. Then reverse your wrist and pull your fingers down toward your forearm. Now find something with a hard edge. Hook your pinkie finger on the edge and reach out with your thumb as far as you can to stretch your wrist and back of the hand. Do this with both hands several times. This is something you can do almost anywhere if you feel your wrists or hands are getting tight or just need a break.

Ankles

While seated on the ground, grab one ankle with one hand and pull back on the ball of your foot with the other hand. Hold this stretched position for at least 20 seconds. Then slowly rotate your foot to the right, to the left, and point it. Repeat with the other ankle. You ankles often get cramped and stiff after long hours in your boat and then make you clumsy as you stumble over seaweed-covered rocks at your landing site. To avoid a turned ankle, always walk between the rocks—especially when you are traveling below the high tide line.

Do gentle wrist stretches in both directions and remember to wiggle your fingers occasionally while you paddle.

TO PEE OR NOT TO PEE

Because of the logistics of having to pee while paddling, many sea kayakers knowingly dehydrate themselves. This is an unhealthy tactic. Women who are encased in wetsuits and drysuits are particularly maladroit at trying to pee while in their cockpit, and they are thus tempted to dehydrate themselves. Men have zippers in all the right places (or at least close to the right places), and their anatomy makes it easier to pee overboard or into a bottle. Crotch zippers for women sea kayakers are quite uncomfortable, since paddling is done from a seated position and most paddling clothing necessitates bulky zippers.

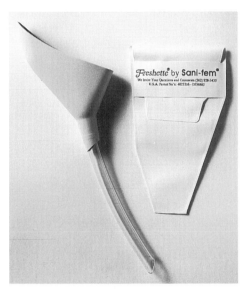

The Freshette by Sani-fem makes it easier to pee while in your cockpit.

Several strategies have been developed by sea kayaking women. I have already mentioned the joys of peeing in your wetsuit while immersed. With the use of the Freshette, a handheld urinary director, you can now pee in the confines of your cockpit (and, like the guys, even write your name in the snow!).

The Freshette is a small cup with a tube attached that you can use to funnel urine into a bottle or a bag for disposal overboard. A wetsuit will still need to be dropped, and paddling pants need to be pulled low. Still, this method beats trying to hang over the side for all to see. You'll need to scooch up to the lip of your seat to have room to pee. But you can always stabilize your boat by using a paddle float outrigger or inflatable sponsons.

More and more women are now ordering their drysuits with men's relief zippers or with drop-seat options, which makes the Freshette easier to use. This same method is useful even on land when the idea of dropping the top half of a drysuit isn't feasible. Make sure your inner layers have access points as well. Buy men's bottoms with a fly or add your own openings.

Heidi Tiura, who has spent a lot of time on the water in everything from kayaks to tugboats, cuts the top of a dishwashing soap container at a handy angle. She suggests using this when you need to urinate in your kayak. But she warns that you should measure how much urine you usually void so the container isn't too small. Heidi also points out, "If the bottle isn't getting warm in your hand, watch out! It went somewhere."

PADDLING WHILE PREGNANT

Several women I talked to raved about the soothing and relaxing effect paddling had on their pregnancies. One paddler said she felt like "an unbalanced slug on land," and the act of floating and paddling created a feeling of weightlessness and ease. For some women, the early stages of pregnancy were actually more difficult because of queasiness. Others had little or no problem with any motion sickness from paddling.

As your body grows in size and its weight distribution is altered through pregnancy, you may need to be aware of slight changes in balance as your center of gravity shifts. Many women felt more comfortable in double kayaks by the middle of the second trimester. They found doubles more comfortable for a number of reasons: They preferred the extra stability of the double; with their growing size, they found entry and exit was easier from the cockpit of a double (and eased their fears of wet reentry); and with less stamina, paddling a double equalized the differences when paddling with others.

By the third trimester, some women noted a decided change in their forward stroke. Torso rotation was minimal, and they had to depend more on their arms, which tired them more easily. By the middle of their third trimester, most women interviewed were restricting themselves to shorter paddles with lots of rest stops built into the outing.

Paddling would seem to be the perfect exercise for pregnant women. It isn't jarring, doesn't cause sudden increases in pulse rates, and it takes stress off the joints such as knees and ankles that often suffer during pregnancy. Any pregnant woman should consult her physician about taking up an exercise regimen or planning a trip out of the range of immediate medical services. Pregnant women should be particularly aware of their need to stay hydrated and keep plenty of water accessible for drinking at all times.

BRING ALONG THE FAMILY

Kayaking is a sport that can involve the whole family or a combination of family members.

When you paddle with family members, make realistic adjustments to your paddling plans and estimated time of travel. Children tire easily when paddling—so don't count on much pull from that quarter! With changing scenery passing by, most children are willing to sit and enjoy the ride for at least an hour or two at a stretch. But you'll need to build in plenty of rest stops and opportunities to get out, stretch, and burn some quick bursts of energy before heading out again. Most parents feel more comfortable having children in the same boat with

Kayaking is a sport for the whole family. Depending on the size of your child, you can share your cockpit, give them a cockpit of their own, or use the center storage compartment on a triple. (Joel Rogers)

PADDLING WITH LILLY

Paddling with a three-and-a-half-year-old means making some adjustments to your own paddling. For Tamsin Venn, being able to share the experience with her daughter makes it all worthwhile. Tamsin's daughter Lilly began kayaking in the middle hatch of a double kayak. Lilly also rode in Tamsin's lap as she paddled a stable single kayak, but Tamsin found it fatiguing to constantly keep her hands high to avoid bonking Lilly on the head.

"I was thrilled when I felt it was safe to put Lilly in the rear hatch [of a single]—feeling confident that she wouldn't jump or wriggle her way out. I thought 'we can really go places now!'" Tamsin and Lilly spent their summer vacation kayaking, launching every day and exploring cove to cove. "It was great," says Tamsin. "We moved slowly and looked at osprey, loons, seaweed, barnacles; touched buoys and rocks when we went by. The most fun was picking up starfish and looking at them in the shallows around the harbor.

"The whole expedition moves very slowly because you need to keep small children entertained by looking at animals and so on. Keep it short—for the boredom factor and the safety factor." Tamsin recommends an hour out and an hour back with plenty of stops along the way to pick up rocks, shells, and other goodies.

Often the family travels with both a double and a single. "Lilly
continued on page 151

them, at least until the children are about seven years of age.

Make sure you invest in a good life vest that is properly sized for your child. Life vests for smaller children (50 pounds or less) and infants will include crotch straps to prevent them from slipping through the vest and a grab handle placed high on the back. Compressions straps around the sides and chest should be snugged up. That way, you can lift a child by the shoulders of her life vest without having the vest slip up around her face. If the vest is comfortable, you won't be faced with a battle before getting on the water. Customize your child's vest with favorite decals or draw something snazzy on the front, along with her name.

Infants and children up to about two years of age are usually content to nestle down in front of you in the cockpit. Often, they are lulled to sleep by the boat's movement. Bring an insulated pad your child can lie on for comfort and warmth. At more active ages, double kayaks with center cockpits are a perfect answer. The kids have their own miniature playground, and you have room to paddle. Even though it's difficult for them to reach the water, giving kids their own paddle (it should be small and light) gets them involved. Make sure to use a paddle leash so you don't have to be a paddle retriever throughout the entire trip.

Many instructional programs offer courses for children, and some programs accept children as young as six years of age. The age at which you begin to teach your children paddling skills is a personal decision. I have seen six-year-olds paddle their

"Josh always fell asleep whenever we took him kayaking, so it was quite easy. The toughest age for us was between two and three years old, when he wanted to investigate everything but couldn't understand being restrained. Now, at six, he has his own small sit-on-top kayak that he paddles in our company. When he gets tired, we hook up a towline and give him a ride!"

—kayaking mom Joan Morrison

"**I** was thrilled when I felt it was safe to put Lilly in the rear hatch [of a single]—feeling confident that she wouldn't jump or wriggle her way out. I thought 'we can really go places now!'"

—Tamsin Venn, kayaking author and publisher of *Atlantic Coastal Kayaker*

own boats tethered to the stern of a parent's boat; when the children get tired, they get a free ride. Being tethered also keeps them from struggling to stay on course if the wind is a factor.

PADDLING WITH A DISABILITY

"When people see me on the water, they can't tell that I'm disabled." That was a point driven home during a Disabled Paddlers Workshop I attended some years ago. Paddling equipment and techniques can be adapted so many people with disabilities can enjoy the same benefits from kayaking that able-bodied paddlers do. For some, a minor adjustment in equipment is all that is required. For others, cockpit adaptations and the accompaniment of an able-bodied paddler are needed. The rewards are significant for everyone involved in the process.

The American Canoe Association (ACA) offers workshops for disabled paddlers. They also train kayak instructors in teaching techniques and equipment adaptation for disabled paddlers. Janet Zeller, president of the ACA and now a disabled paddler, has inspired and energized this movement along with many others. These programs have created exciting opportunities for disabled paddlers. Kayak instructors have also been able to broaden their understanding of paddling skills and enhance their teaching abilities.

A significant portion of the population (at last estimate, approximately 25 percent) is disabled. Since the range of disabilities is huge—encompassing visual, hearing, mental, and physical impairments—adaptations are varied. If you are disabled and plan to paddle, you should approach the sport the same way an able-bodied paddler would. You should seek a professional instruction program that has instructors experienced in adapting kayaking

continued from page 150

sometimes travels from boat to boat—we raft up and she makes the exchange into another hatch. When the wind comes up, she goes underneath." Tamsin cautions that you'll need to rethink your packing for overnights when you're dealing with a passenger in one of the hatches!

Tamsin dresses Lilly for immersion in a wetsuit, thermal underwear, PFD, surf shoes, whistle, wide-brimmed hat, sunglasses with string, and lots of sunscreen. She packs a set of spare clothes and lots of snacks and drinks. Lilly has her own paddle; "patience is required when Lilly tries to bash our paddles together or rudder . . . or leans to one side, threatening a capsize."

When paddling with children, Tamsin cautions, "stay close to shore. It will be easier to get out for a quick stretch or for any emergency." And don't forget to sing: "Anything repetitive. It will buy a little more paddling time. A loon imitation helps!"

By the next paddling season, Lilly will be too big for a rear hatch. She's getting her own kayak to play around with on protected water. "It's fun to be sharing the water environment with Lilly, and I feel I'm instilling future enjoying of the outdoors. But as one person said to me, when she grows up she's either going to love or loathe paddling. Wait and see!"

—Portions of this sidebar reprinted from "Lilly Goes to Moosehead Lake" by Tamsin Venn, *Atlantic Coastal Kayaker*, August 1997.

• •

"I was very nervous trying kayaking. I couldn't imagine how I could do it, but I wanted to try. I'm a paraplegic. My instructor padded out the entire cockpit in a double and blocked in my legs and feet with foam (I have to be very careful about pinching and bruising). The double was great, but I couldn't wait to try my own boat—to have just me in charge. After some practice in a pool and two outings in a protected harbor in the double with my instructor, I got my chance! It was fantastic.

"I'm getting my own boat and fixing it up just for me. Sometimes the logistics seem a bit overwhelming, but once I'm on the water I forget all the other stuff. It's a great feeling."

—new paddler Lisa Erickson

• •

equipment for your use. A list of instructors who have been trained through the ACA Disabled Paddlers Program is maintained by the ACA. If instructional programs are not familiar with this program, you should urge them to get involved.

Kayaking equipment can be adapted for paddlers with disabilities. (Courtesy of Environmental Traveling Companions)

Chapter 10

RESOURCES

A ll of these listings have proven valuable to me as a sea kayaker. There are many more resources for paddlesports in general and a host of related topics that could fill an entire book (in fact they have: Zip Kellogg's *The Whole Paddler's Catalog*, Ragged Mountain Press, 1997). Enjoy these listings, expand your horizons, and keep a sharp eye out for other sources.

Books

OTHER "HOW-TO" BOOKS ON SEA KAYAKING

The Bombproof Roll and Beyond by Paul Dutky, Menasha Ridge Press, 1993

Canoeing and Kayaking: Instruction Manual by Laurie Gullion, et al, edited by Thomas Foster, American Canoe Association, 1987

Canoeing and Kayaking for Persons with Physical Disabilities by Anne Wortham Webre and Janet A. Zeller, edited by Laurie Gullion, American Canoe Association, 1990

Canoeing Handbook: Official Handbook of the British Canoe Union edited by Ray Rowe, The Chameleon Press Limited, 1990

The Complete Book of Sea Kayaking by Derek C. Hutchinson, The Globe Pequot Press, 1995

Complete Folding Kayaker by Ralph Diaz, Ragged Mountain Press, 1994

Complete Sea Kayak Touring by Jonathon Hanson, Ragged Mountain Press, 1998

The Coastal Kayaker's Manual: The Complete Guide to Skills, Gear, and Sea Sense by Randel Washburne, The Globe Pequot Press, 1993

Eskimo Rolling by Derek C. Hutchinson, Ragged Mountain Press, 1992

The Essential Sea Kayaker: A Complete Course for the Open Water Paddler by David Seidman, Ragged Mountain Press, 1992

Guide to Expedition Kayaking on Sea and Open Water by Derek C. Hutchinson, The Globe Pequot Press, 1995

Hearst Marine Books Kayak Camping by David Harrison, William Morrow & Co., 1996

Hearst Marine Books Sea Kayaking Basics by David Harrison, William Morrow & Co., 1993

Sea Kayaking by Nigel Foster, The Globe Pequot Press, 1990

Sea Kayaking: A Manual for Long-Distance Touring by John Dowd, University of Washington Press, 1997

SEAMANSHIP, WEATHER, AND THE OCEAN

Chapman Piloting: Seamanship and Small Boat Handling, 62nd edition, by Elbert S. Maloney, William Morrow & Co., 1996

Fundamentals of Kayak Navigation by David Burch, The Globe Pequot Press, 1993

Navigational Rules: International-Inland, Gordon Press, 1997

Sea Kayaker's Deep Trouble: True Stories and Their Lessons from Sea Kayaker Magazine by Matt Broze and George Gronseth, edited by Christopher Cunningham, Ragged Mountain Press, 1997

Weather for the Mariner by William J. Kotsch, Naval Institute Press, 1983

Waves and Beaches by Willard Bascom, Doubleday, 1980

BUILD YOUR OWN KAYAK

The Aleutian Kayak by Wolfgang Brink, Ragged Mountain Press, 1995

The Kayak Shop: Three Elegant Wooden Kayaks Anyone Can Build by Chris Kulczycki, Ragged Mountain Press, 1993

Wood and Canvas Kayak Building by George Putz, Ragged Mountain Press, 1990

HISTORY AND TRADITIONAL DESIGN

Baidarka: The Kayak by George Dyson, Alaska Northwest Publishing Company, 1986

The Bark Canoes and Skin Boats of North America by Edwin Tappan Adney and Howard I. Chapelle, The Smithsonian Institution, 1983

Qajaq: Kayaks of Siberia and Alaska by David W. Zimmerly, University of Washington Press, 1986

The Starship and the Canoe by Kenneth Brower, HarperCollins, 1983

TRAVEL AND ADVENTURE BY KAYAK

A Boat in Our Baggage: Around the World with a Kayak by Maria Coffey, Ragged Mountain Press, 1995

Alone at Sea by Hannes Lindemann, Polner Verlag, 1992

Deep Water Passage: A Spiritual Journey at Midlife by Ann Linnea, Little Brown and Co., 1995

Good Food for Camp & Trail: All-Natural Recipes for Delicious Meals Outdoors by Dorcas S. Miller, Pruett Publishing, 1993

Kayak Cookery by Linda Daniel, Menasha Ridge Press, 1997

The Happy Isles of Oceania: Paddling the Pacific by Paul Theroux, Ballantine Books, 1993

The Hidden Coast by Joel W. Rogers, Alaska Northwest Books, 1991

Hot Showers! Maine Coast Lodgings for Kayakers and Sailors by Lee Bumsted, Biddle Publishing Co., 1997

Island Paddling: A Paddler's Guide to the Gulf Islands and Barkley Sound by Mary Ann Snowden, Orca Book Publishers, 1990

Kayaking Puget Sound, the San Juans & Gulf Islands: 45 Trips on the Northwest's Inland Waters by Randel Washburne, Mountaineers Books, 1990

Rivers Running Free: A Century of Women's Canoeing Adventures edited by Judith Niemi and Barbara Wieser, Seal Press, 1997

Paddling My Own Canoe by Audrey Sutherland, University of Hawaii Press, 1978

Paddling the Sunshine Coast by Dorothy and Bodhi Drope, Harbour Publishing, 1997

Sea Kayaking along the Mid-Atlantic Coast by Tamsin Venn, Appalachian Mountain Club Books, 1994

Sea Kayaking along the New England Coast by Tamsin Venn, Appalachian Mountain Club Books, 1990

Sea Kayaking in Baja by Andromeda Romano-Lax, Wilderness Press, 1993

Seekers of the Horizon edited by Will Nordby, The Globe Pequot Press, 1989

WILDERNESS MEDICINE

Hypothermia: The Basic Essentials by William W. Forgey, M.D., ICS Books, 1991

Medicine for the Backcountry by Buck Tilton and Frank Hubbell, ICS Books, 1994

The Onboard Medical Handbook by Paul Gill, M.D., Ragged Mountain Press, 1997

The Outward Bound Wilderness First-Aid Handbook by Peter Goth and Jeffrey Isaac, Lyons and Burford, 1991

LOW-IMPACT TECHNIQUE

Backwoods Ethics: Environmental Issues for Hikers and Campers by Laura and Guy Waterman, Countryman Press, 1993

How to Shit in the Woods by Kathleen Meyer, Ten Speed Press, 1994

Leave No Trace: Outdoor Skills and Ethics–Temperate Coastal Zones, National Outdoor Leadership School, Lander, WY, 800-332-4100

Soft Paths: How to Enjoy the Wilderness Without Harming It by Bruce Hampton and David Cole, Stackpole Books, 1988

REPAIR AND MAINTENANCE

The Essential Outdoor Gear Manual by Annie Getchell, Ragged Mountain Press, 1995

Magazines

Atlantic Coastal Kayaker, Ipswich, MA, 508-356-6112

Canoe and Kayak Magazine, Kirkland, WA, 425-827-6363

Folding Kayaker, New York, NY, 212-724-5069

Paddler, Eagle, ID, 703-455-3419
Sea Kayaker, Seattle, WA, 206-789-9536

Videos

Performance Sea Kayaking: The Basics and Beyond by Kent Ford Performance Video and Instruction, 550 Riverbend, Durango, CO 81301 (303-259-1361)

Surf Kayaking Fundamentals by John Lull, P.O. Box 564, El Granada, CA 94018, 650-726-7202

What Now? Sea Kayak Rescue Techniques by Vaughan Smith and Shelley Johnson, Powerface, 1448 West Appleton Road, Appleton, ME 04862

Internet sources

Most kayak manufacturers and many of the larger outfitters have their own websites. While there are too many to list here, the addresses can be found in manufacturers' ads, in paddling magazines, or through online searches. The following noncommercial resources may provide links to a variety of other kayaking pages.

California Kayak Friends: www.ckf.org
GORP (Great Outdoors Recreation Pages): www.gorp.com
Paddler's newsgroup: rec.boats.paddle
Tide and Current Predictor: tbone.biol.sc.edu/tide/sitesel.html

Kayaking instruction and travel

There are numerous outfitters and paddlesports shops that offer guided trips and instructional programs for sea kayaking. Some specialize in women's programs, others offer a mix of classes for both women and men. Rather than offer a comprehensive list here and hope that it would remain accurate, I urge you to peruse paddlesports magazines for the multitude of listings they offer and request as many brochures as you would like to receive. You can also contact the Trade Association of Paddlesports (414-242-5228) for recommendations.

Many of the women who have supported this book and are quoted in its text offer excellent instructional programs and tours for all levels:

Joanne Turner of Southwind Kayak Center (Irvine, CA), 800-SOUTHWIND
Judy Moyer of Pacific Water Sports (Seattle, WA), 206-246-9385
Linda Legg, BCU instructor (Everglades, FL), LLKayaker@worldnet.att.net
Deb Shapiro of The Kayak Centre (Wickford, RI), 888-SEA-KAYAK
Cheryl Levin of Maine Sport Outfitters (Rockport, ME), 800-722-0826
Pam Sweeney of Winnipesaukee Kayak (Wolfeboro, NH), 603-569-9926

Equipment sources

Several companies have proven especially helpful to the women's paddlesports market as well as this book. In many cases, these companies donated products for field testing during the research phase of this book. Happily, more and more products that are particularly useful for women paddlers are entering the marketplace every year.

Current Designs (kayaks and paddles)
10124 McDonald Park Road
Sidney, BC Canada V8L 3X9
Phone (250) 655-1822
http://www.cdkayak.com

Deep See/Warmers (wetsuits)
18935 59th Avenue NE
Arlington, WA 98223
Phone (800) 367-0440

Dr. D Paddles
80 Second Street
South Portland, ME 04106
Phone (800) 295-0042
http://www.wowpages.com/malone

Kokatat (paddlewear)
5350 Ericson Way
Arcata, CA 95521
Phone (800) 225-9749

MTI (life vests)
PO Box 1045
Watertown, MA 02272
Phone (800) 783-4684

Ocean Kayak (sit-on-top kayaks)
PO Box 5003
Ferndale, WA 98248
Phone (800) 8KAYAKS
http://www.oceankayak.com

Paddle Boy Designs (kayak carts)
1407 Park Avenue
Winona Lake, IN 46590
Phone (219) 268-0081
http://www.paddleboy.com

Sani-Fem Company (Freshette)
PO Box 4117
Downey, CA 90241
Phone (800) 542-5580

Seattle Sports Company (dry bags, paddle floats)
1415 NW 52nd Street
Seattle, WA 98107
Phone (800) 632-6616

Yakima (HullyRollers)
PO Drawer 4899
Arcata, CA 95518
Phone (800) 348-9232
http://www.yakima.com

General outdoor courses and networking

Becoming an Outdoors-Woman
Dr. Christine Thomas
College of Natural Resources
University of Wisconsin–Stevens Point
Stevens Point, WI 54481
Phone (715) 346-4185
http://www.state.nj.us/dep/fgw/bowhome.htm

National Outdoor Leadership School
288 Main Street
Lander, WY 82520
Phone (307) 332-6973
Phone for Leave No Trace (800) 332-4100
Fax (307) 332-1220
email: admissions@nols.edu
http://www.nols.edu/

Women's Outdoor Network
PO Box 50003
Palo Alto, CA 94303
Phone (650) 494-8583
Fax (650) 712-9093
email: wonforfun@earthlink.net
http://home.earthlink.net/~wonforfun/

Women's Sports Foundation
Eisenhower Park
East Meadow, NY 11554
Phone (800) 227-3988, (516) 542-4700
Fax (516) 542-4716
email: wosport@aol.com
http://www.lifetimetv.com/WoSport

Women's Wellness

The Melpomene Institute
1010 University Avenue
St. Paul, MN 55104
Phone (612) 642-1951
Fax (612) 642-1871
email: melpomen@skypoint.com
http://www.melpomene.org

Paddling events

Alaska Sea Kayak Symposium, Anchorage, AK, 907-564-8314
Annual Ocean Kayak Festival, Victoria, British Columbia, 250-247-9789
Captiva Sea kayak Classic and Symposium, Captiva Island, FL 414-242-5228

Delmarva Paddlesports Expo, Salisbury, MD 410-543-1244
Coastal Kayak Symposium, Thetis Island, British Columbia, 604-597-1122
East Coast Canoe & Kayak Symposium, Charleston, SC, 803-762-2172
Georgian Bay Sea Kayak Symposium, Nobel, Ontario, 705-342-5324
Great Lakes Sea Kayak Symposium, Grand Marais, MI, 248-683-4770
Inland Sea Society Symposium, Bayfield, WI 715-373-0674
Jersey Canoe Club Sea Kayaking Symposium, Jersey, British Channel Islands, 011-44-15346-39390
L.L. Bean Atlantic Coast Sea Kayak Symposium. Held in mid-July in Castine, ME, 800-221-4221 Ext. 26666
Shetland Sea Kayak Symposium, Muckle Roe, Shetland, Scotland 011-44-01950-422-325
Southwestern Canoe Rendezvous, Houston, TX 713-373-0674
Trade Association of Paddlesports (TAPS) hosts several Sea Kayak Symposia every year on both coasts and in the Great Lakes region. Dates and exact

locations change, so it is best to keep an eye out in paddlesports magazines' calendars or call the Trade Association of Paddlesports at 414-242-5228.

Other resources

American Canoe Association
7432 Alban Station Blvd., Suite B-226
Springfield, VA 22150-2311
703-451-0141

British Canoe Union
John Dudderidge House
Adbolton Lane
West Bridgford, Nottingham NG2 5AS
England

North American Water Trails, Inc.
c/o S. Rumble
24130 NW Johnson Road
Poulsbo, WA 98370
360-697-3484

• •

North American paddling clubs

ALASKA

Juneau Kayak Club
PO Box 021865
Juneau, AK 99802-1865

ARIZONA

Desert Paddling Association
620 E. 19th Street, Suite 110
Tucson, AZ 85719

Southern Arizona Paddling Club
PO Box 77185
Tucson, AZ 85703

BRITISH COLUMBIA

Alliance of British Columbia Sea Kayak Guides
221 Ferntree Place
Nanaimo, BC V9R 5M1

Cowichan Kayak and Canoe Club
5086 McLay Road, RR #3
Duncan, BC V9L 2X1

Ocean Kayak Association of British Columbia
106 Payne Road
Box 15
Saturna Island, BC V0N 2Y0

Royal Bamfield Kayak & Yacht Club
Box 32
Bamfield, BC V0R 1B0

Sea Kayak Association of British Columbia
Box 751 Postal Station A
Vancouver, BC V6C 2N6

Victoria Sea Kayakers' Network
752 Victoria Avenue
Victoria, BC V8S 4N3

CALIFORNIA

California Kayak Friends
Suite A 199, 14252 Culver Dr.
Irvine, CA 92714

Environmental Traveling Companions (ETC)
Ft. Mason Center
Landmark Building C
San Francisco, CA 94123

Miramar Beach Kayak Club
Number One Mirada Road
Half Moon Bay, CA 94019

San Diego Paddling Club
1829 Chalcedony Street
San Diego, CA 92109

San Francisco Bay Area Sea Kayakers
229 Courtright Road
San Rafael, CA 94901

Slackwater Yacht Club
B37 Gate 6 Road
Sausalito, CA 94965

Western Sea Kayakers
PO Box 59436
San Jose, CA 95159

COLORADO

Rocky Mountain Sea Kayak Club

PO Box 100643
Denver, CO 80210

CONNECTICUT

CONN-YAK
PO Box 2006
Branford, CT 06405

Nordkapp Owners' Club of America
47 Argyle Avenue
West Hartford, CT 06107

FLORIDA

Central Florida Paddle Masters
2460 Avenue E SW
Winter Haven, FL 33880

Coconut Kayakers
PO Box 3646
Tequesta, FL 33469

Emerald Coast Paddlers
7 Bayshore Point
Valparaiso, FL 32580

Florida Sea Kayaking Association
9529 Kuhn Road
Jacksonville, FL 32257

Tampa Bay Sea Kayakers
PO Box 12263
St. Petersburg, FL 33713-
2263

West Florida Canoe Club
PO Box 17203
Pensacola, FL 32522

HAWAII

Hawaii Island Kayak Club
74-425 Keal a Kehe Parkway
Kailua-Kana, HI 96740

Hui W'a Kaukahi
c/o Go Bananas
732 Kapahula Avenue
Honolulu, HI 96816

Kanaka Ikaika Racing Club
PO Box 438
Kaneohe, HI 96744

Maui Outing Club
c/o Maui Outdoor Center
PO Box 277-330
Maui, HI 96753

ILLINOIS

Chicago Area Sea Kayakers
4019 N. Narragansett
Chicago, IL 60634

**Saukenuk Paddlers' Canoe
and Kayak Club**
PO Box 1038
Moline, IL 61265

LOUISIANA

**Bayou Haystackers Canoe
and Kayak Club**
c/o Hans W. Brandl
8744 Forest Hill
Baton Rouge, LA 70809

**Gulf Coast Open Water
Kayaking Association**
1640 Harbor Drive, Suite 123
Sidell, LA 70458

MAINE

Portsmouth Kayak Club
56 Eliot Road
Kittery, ME 03904

**Southern Maine Sea
Kayaking Network**
PO Box 4794
Portland, ME 04112

MANITOBA

**Big Lake Kayak Touring
Club**
c/o Phil Manaigre
401 Ash Street
Winnipeg, MB R3N 0P8

MARYLAND

**Chesapeake Paddler's
Association**
PO Box 341
Greenbelt, MD 20768

**Tantallon International Sea
Kayaking Association**
12308 Loch Carron Circle
Fort Washington, MD 20744

MASSACHUSETTS

Boston Sea Kayak Club
47 Nancy Road
Newton, MA 02167

**Cape Ann Rowing and
Kayak Club**
PO Box 1715
Gloucester, MA 01931-1715

**Martha's Vineyard Oar &
Paddle**
PO Box 840
West Tisbury, MA 02575

North Shore Kayakers
PO Box 50
Marblehead, MA 01945

Roofrack Yacht Club
113 Railroad Avenue
Hamilton, MA 01982

MICHIGAN

**Great Lakes Sea Kayaking
Club**
3721 Shallow Brook
Bloomfield Hills, MI 48013

International Klepper Society
PO Box 973
Good Hart, MI 49737

**Lansing Oar and Paddle
Club**
PO Box 26254
Lansing, MI 48909

Negwegon Kayak Club
218 West Bay Street
East Tawas, MI 48703

**West Michigan Coastal
Kayakers' Association**
c/o Karl Geisel
923 Griggs SE
Grand Rapids, MI 49507-
2731

MINNESOTA

**Twin Cities Sea Kayaking
Association**
PO Box 581792
Minneapolis, MN 55458-
1792

**University of Minnesota
Kayak Club**
108 Kirby Student Center
The University of Min-
nesota–Duluth
10 University Drive
Duluth, MN 55812-2496

**Upper Midwest Kayak
Touring News**
PO Box 17115
Minneapolis, MN 55417-
0115

MISSOURI

**Great River Paddle Touring
Society**
334 S. Marguerite
St. Louis, MO 63135

MONTANA

Flathead Paddlers
15 18th Street E
Kalispell, MT 59901

**Ocean & River Kayaking
Adventures**
355 Boon Road
Somers, MT 59932

NEW JERSEY

**Jersey Shore Association of
Sea Kayakers**
159 Fells Road
Essex Fells, NJ 07021-1614

Seabright Paddle Association
c/o Debbie Reeves
200 Monmouth Avenue
Atlantic Highland, NJ 07716

**South Jersey Sea Kayaker's
Association**
123 Heathercroft
Egg Harbor Township, NJ
08234

NEW YORK

Adirondack Mountain Club
Genesee Valley Chapter
47 Thorpe Crescent
Rochester, NY 14616

FLOW Paddlers Club
4300 Canandaigua Road
Walworth, NY 14568

Huntington Kayak Klub
51 Central Parkway
Huntington, NY 11743-4308

**Metropolitan Association of
Sea Kayakers**
195 Prince Street, Basement
New York, NY 10012

**Metropolitan Canoe and
Kayak Club**
PO Box 021868
Brooklyn, NY 11202-0040

Sebago Canoe Club
Paerdegat Basin
Foot of Avenue N
Brooklyn, NY 11236

Touring Kayak Club
205 Beach Street
City Island, Bronx, NY
10464

ONTARIO

**Great Lakes Sea Kayaking
Association**
PO Box 22082
45 Overlea Boulevard
Toronto, ON M4H 1N9

Ottawa Sea Kayaking Club
5-968 Byron Avenue
Ottawa, ON K2A 0J3

OREGON

BUNSAW
112 West 18th Place
Eugene, OR 97402

**Oregon Ocean Paddling
Society (OOPS)**
PO Box 69641
Portland, OR 97201

PENNSYLVANIA

ANorAK
5926 Ridge Avenue
Philadelphia, PA 19128

Pittsburgh Council AYH
6300 Fifth Avenue
Pittsburgh, PA 15232

SOUTH CAROLINA

SandLapper Sea Yackers
525 Longbranch Road
Gilbert, SC 29054

TEXAS

Houston Canoe Club
PO Box 925516
Houston, TX 77292-5516

Texas Sea Touring Kayak
Club
PO Box 27281
Houston, TX 77227

VERMONT

Champlain Kayak Club
89 Caroline Street
Burlington, VT 05401

VIRGINIA

Association of North
Atlantic Kayakers
34 East Queens Way
Hampton, VA 23669

WASHINGTON

Baidarka Historical Society
PO Box 5454
Bellingham, WA 98227

Eddyline Paddling Club
3037 46th Avenue SW
Seattle, WA 98116-3312

Lesbian and Gay Sea
Kayakers
1202 E. Pike #896
Seattle, WA 98122-3934

Mountaineers
300 3rd Avenue W
Seattle, WA 98119

North Sound Sea Kayaking
Association (NSSKA)
PO Box 1523
Everett, WA 98206

Olympic Kayak Club
22293 Clear Creek Road NW
Poulsbo, WA 98370

Port Orchard Paddle Club
2398 Jefferson Avenue SE
Port Orchard, WA 98366

Puget Sound Paddle Club
PO Box 111892
Tacoma, WA 98411-1892

Seattle Sea Kayaking Club
13906 123rd Avenue NE
Kirkland, WA 98034-2247

Washington Kayak Club
PO Box 24264
Seattle, WA 98124

Whatcom Association of
Kayak Enthusiasts
(WAKE)
PO Box 1952
Bellingham, WA 98227
6Yakima Kayak Club
PO Box 11147
Yakima, WA 98909

WISCONSIN

RASKA
4805 S. Lakeshore Drive
Racine, WI 53403-4127

Overseas paddling clubs

Association De Kayak De
Mer Du Ponant
60 Rue Xavier Graal
29500 Ergue Gaberic,
Brittany, France

Auckland Sea Kayak
Network
c/o Vincent Maire
7 Mouora Road
Whangaparaoa, New Zealand
1463

Brunnsvikens Kanotklubb
Frescati Hagvag 5
S-104 05
Stockholm, Sweden

Canterbury Sea Kayaker's
Network
c/o Alex Ferguson
12 Dunn St.
Christchurch, New Zealand

Carribean Kayaking Alliance
Kayaker's Point
Inch Marlowe, Barbados

Causeway Coast Kayak
Association
12 Glenvale Avenue
Portrush, County Antrim
North Ireland BT56 8HL

CK/Mer–Connaissance du
Kayak de Mer
BP 67B, 22500
Paimpol, Brittany, France

Grenland Havpadleklubb–
Telemark Coast
c/o Sigmund Hansen
Skaugaardsgt 31
N-3970 Langesund, Norway

Helsingin Melojat
Kapylantie 1 C 42
00610 Finland

Il Kayak da Mare
c/o Sergio Cadoni
Viale Colombo 118
09045 Quartu S.
Elena, Cagliari, Italy

International Sea Kayaking
Association
5 Osprey Avenue
The Hoskers, Westhoughton
Bolton, Lancashire, England
Bl5 2SL

Investigator Canoe Club
c/o 28 Rowells Road
Lockleys, South Australia
5032

Jersey Canoe Club
c/o Kevin Mansell
177 Quennejais Park,
St. Brelade, Jersey, JE38JU
British Isles

Kanu Verein Unterweser
c/o Wolfgang Bisle
Tidemanstr. 37
D-28759 Bremen, Germany

Kiwi Association of Sea
Kayakers N.Z. Inc
c/o Paul Caffyn
RD 1
Runanga, West Coast, New
Zealand

Mar del Plata Kayak Club
c/o Adrian Pol
Ayacucho 3108
7600 Mar Del Plata,
Argentina

Melaveikot r.y.
c/o Matti Seppanen
Maistraatinkatu 6 C 15
00240, Helsinki, Finland

NSW Sea Kayak Club Inc.
29 Westgarth Street
O'Connor ACT 2602
Australia

Paddlers International
8 Wilstshire Avenue
Hornchurch, Essex, England
RM11 3DX

Peddelpraat
p/a Ine Dost
Duivenkamp 726
NL-3607 VD Maarssen,
The Netherlands

Salzwasserunion
c/o Bernhard Hillejan
Karl-Arnold-Stasse 10
D-51109 Koln, Germany

Sea Kayak Group UK
c/o John Fiszman
54 St. Clare's Close
Littleover, Derby, England
DE22 3JF

Sea Kayak Operators'
Association (NZ)
c/o PO Box 195
Picton, New Zealand

Shetland Canoe Club
c/o Bridge-end Outdoor
Centre
Bridge-end, Burra Isle,
Shetland ZE2 9LE

Stavanger Kajakklubb
c/o Torbjorn Evensen
Professor Hansteens gt. 27
4021 Stavanger, Norway

Tasmanian Sea Canoeing
Club
PO Box 599F
Hobart, Tasmania, Australia
7001

Victoria Sea Kayak Club
154 Waterdale Road
Ivanhoe, Victoria, Australia
3079

Index

A

American Canoe Association (ACA), 19, 152
assisted reentry. *See* reentry techniques

B

back stroke, 44–45
Beaufort Scale, 114–115. *See also* wind
bilge pump, 59–60, 93
    for assisted reentry, 67
    for doubles, 66, 73
    for solo reentry, 64
    storage, 60
boat repair kit, 107
braces (support strokes), 49–52
    head dink, 51
British Canoe Union (BCU), 19
bulkheads, 28, 83–84
    in assisted reentry, 69
    resealing, 108
buoys, 136 (illustration)
    channel, 132–133
    in fog, 128
    numbering, 136

C

carrying your boat, 25, 30–32
carts (trolleys), 31–32
charts, nautical, 135–137
chine, 87
clapotis, 112–113
clothing for paddling, 99–102
    cold water protection, 21, 99–101
    for instructional programs, 19
    storage of, 104–105
cockpit, 28
    adjustment and fitting, 29–30, 85
    coaming, 29
    customizing, 30, 88–89
    emptying of water, 64, 69
communication
    during assisted reentry, 67, 73
    foghorn signals, 94
    paddle signals, 130
    VHF, 96–97
    whistle signals, 94, 128
compass (deck), 25, 28, 85, 134
compass rose, 137
composite boats, 80–81
    repair, 105–106
contact lenses, 102
customizing (for fit), 88–89

D

deck rigging, 28–29, 84–85
    during assisted reentry, 71
    for safety equipment, 59, 60
    during solo reentry, 62
disabled paddlers, 151–152
    adapting equipment, 20
    choice of boat, 23
    instructional programs, 152
    reentry techniques, 72–73
dehydration/hydration, 24, 101, 148
    when pregnant, 149
double kayak, 88
    for couple, 16
    order of reentry, 65–66
    reentry techniques, 65–66, 73
    sit-on-top, 15
draw strokes, 52–55
dry bags, 19, 102

E

eddies, 122–123
    at the stern, 117
    in the ocean, 122–123
Eskimo roll, 74–77

F

feathering (paddle), 41–42
flotation bags, 83–84
folding kayaks, 81–82
forward stroke, 42–44
    course corrections during, 109–110

G

gelcoat, 81
    repair, 105–106
getting in and out
    from land, 35–37
    in surf, 36
    from the water. *See* reentry techniques
GPS, 138
guided trips, 14–15, 21–22

H

head dink, 51
hypothermia, 99–101

I

inflatable kayaks, 82–83
instructional programs, 18, 21
    all-women's, 20

    for disabled paddlers, 152
    instructor certifications, 19
    for kids, 150
    questions to ask, 19, 21
    for rolling, 74

J

J-lean, 37–38. *See also* leaning your boat

K

kayak design, 79, 86
    beam, 86–87, 92
    chine, 87
    fit, 78–79, 87, 88–89
    hull cross sections, 87
    length, 87, 27
Kevlar, 80–81, 82
kids and kayaking, 15, 149–150
knots, 33

L

leaning your boat, 37–38
    during assisted reentry, 67
    during sweep stroke, 45–49
    to shorten waterline, 46, 84
life vests, 60, 93, 97
    kids, 150
loading kayak on car
    cradles, 32, 35
    loading, 25, 32–35
    perils, 104
    tying down, 33–34
low-impact technique, 143–144

M

maintenance and storage, 25–26, 103–105
    drysuit gaskets, 104
    kayak, 103–104
    neoprene, 104–105
    paddle, 104
    waterproof clothing, 104–105

N

nautical charts, 135–137
navigational tools, 135–138

P

packing, 140–142
    boat trim, 141
    storage compartments, 28–29

paddle blades, 40, 91
  design, 90–92
  leading edge, 46–47
  orientation, 41
  for support, 45, 49
paddle float, 59–60, 93
  for doubles, 66
  for learning to roll, 77
  in solo reentry, 61–64
  storage, 60
paddle leash, 70, 93
paddle strokes (general), 41–42
paddles, 40, 91
  feathered vs. unfeathered, 41–42
  feather angle, 41–42, 90
  grip, 40–41
  length, 40, 92
  materials, 90
  purchasing, 90
  signaling with, 130
  spare, 90, 92
  storage, 104
  take-apart, 40, 90
  weight, 92–93
paddling at night, 95–96
polyethylene boats, 80
  repair, 107–108
pump. *See* bilge pump
purchasing a kayak, 38, 82, 90–91

R

radio, VHF, 85, 95, 96–97
ranges, 139–140
recreational kayaks, 79, 88–89
reentry techniques, 56, 61–74
  assisted, 66–74
  doubles, 65–66, 73
  gear for, 59–60
  practicing, 56, 65

  with rescue sling, 64–65
  solo, 61–65
repairs, 103, 105–108
rescues, 61–73
rescue sling, 59–60, 93
  knots for, 33
  storage, 60
  use of, 64–65, 67, 72
rolling. *See* Eskimo roll
rudder systems, 29
  cables, 70
  to combat weathercocking, 118
  in doubles, 88
  drawbacks, 84
  protection when loading, 32–34
  rudder lines, 29, 61
  versus skegs, 84–85
rules of the road, 132–133

S

scoop rescue, 72–73
seasickness, 26
seating, 29–30
signaling devices, 94–97
sit-on-top kayaks, 15, 19, 89, 131–132
skegs, 84, 85
skin on frame kayaks, 83
solo reentry. *See* reentry techniques
speed, 120, 121, 137
sprayskirts, 57, 58, 98
stern rudder strokes, 55
strength, 23–24, 38, 72
stretching, 145–147
strokes, 41–55
  back stroke, 44–45
  braces (support strokes), 49–52
  draw strokes, 52–55
  forward stroke, 42–44
  paddle strokes (general), 41–42

  stern rudder strokes, 55
  support strokes, 49–52
  sweep (turning) strokes, 45–49
sun protection, 102–103
  for your boat, 25,103,104
surf zone, 129–132
sweep (turning) strokes
  boat lean, 45–46
  combinations, 49
  forward sweep, 46–48
  reverse sweep, 48–49

T

thighbraces, 29
tides, 118–122
toggles, carrying, 28, 30
towing, 98–99
T rescues, 68–72
trip plans, 127–128, 141–142, 144
turning your boat. *See* sweep strokes

V

VHF radio, 85, 95, 96–97

W

waterline length, 27, 87
water trails, 142–143
waves, 110–113
weather, 123–129
weathercocking, 117–118
wind
  as tormentor, 24
  Beaufort Scale, 114–115
  paddling in, 115–118
  speed and direction, 113–114
  veering and backing, 125
wrist alignment, 42, 44
  stretches, 147